In memory of Sylvia, a former 'Miss Manchester'

SAY GOODBYE TO JIMMY BROWN

James Stanhope-Brown

Published by New Generation Publishing in 2016

Copyright © James Stanhope-Brown 2016

Front cover: Jimmy Brown and Sylvia

First Edition

The author asserts the moral right under the Copyright, Designs and Patents Act 1988 to be identified as the author of this work.

All Rights reserved. No part of this publication may be reproduced, stored in a retrieval system or transmitted, in any form or by any means without the prior consent of the author, nor be otherwise circulated in any form of binding or cover other than that which it is published and without a similar condition being imposed on the subsequent purchaser.

www.newgeneration-publishing.com

New Generation Publishing

FOREWORD

Say Goodbye to Jimmy Brown is a story based on fact. It is an unusual story that occurs during the 1950's era when, as a teenager, the author James Stanhope-Brown embraced not only a new beginning but also a new identity.

Disadvantaged from the start, owing to an isolated and institutionalised upbringing in a sometimes cruel children's home, Jimmy rejoins society with a naivety and innocence befitting that of a young child on his first day at school – only instead of a satchel filled with pencils and books, he carries a shoulder bag full of anxious thoughts and feelings of inadequacy.

Using snatches of memory to instigate each episode of the story, the author describes his teenage years and beyond, when he tried desperately to fit in with society without making any faux pas and without drawing attention to himself. We also witness his developing relationships and, indeed, his own identity and self-confidence developing throughout the story.

Running alongside his own story, the author relates the tumultuous story of his beautiful sister, whose looks are admired far and wide. Encouraged by her adopted family, the Seymours, she achieves notoriety and fame as a beauty contestant

When Jimmy is adopted by the same family as his sister, we gradually discover the manipulative and devious nature of his new mother. It becomes clear that Jimmy's promotion to that of an adopted son has come at a price, and he realises he's nothing but a pacifier in an ongoing battle of wills between his sister and his domineering mother. In fact, it's Mrs Seymour's desperation to control every aspect of Jimmy and Sylvia's life that finally tears the family apart.

In an attempt to close a chapter on an unsavoury and troubled part of his life, the author not only delves into a trauma-ridden and institutionalised childhood, he sheds light on a later time that was responsible for influencing, if not haunting, him for the rest of his life.

INTRODUCTION

During the late Victorian era and as a result of a momentous decision by a Northern city's board of guardians, a countryside colony was founded for the purpose of raising children who were either orphaned or in need of care. In their wisdom, taking into account the polluted, industrial conditions of that period, the guardians viewed the scheme as being the best possible alternative to either the workhouse or the fostering arrangements that existed at the time. There would be many benefits for a growing girl or boy, they agreed, including clean air, a rural environment and a complete break from all the bad influences of their past lives.

By providing a school and a church, together with a variety of workshops, the colony became self-sufficient; indeed, from the children's point of view, it became cut off from the world, seemingly miles and miles from any other form of civilisation.

By providing an education and tuition in basic life skills, it was assumed that every boy and girl would eventually rejoin society as ambassadors of a unique and successful system of child welfare; or, in the words of the guardians themselves, "Having learned the basics of life – including having been taught to be God-fearing and obedient servants, when they are ready, they – the older ones – will then go out into the world, to face life as fully confident and able-bodied combatants."

And so it was, in the year 1936, a certain two-year-old boy by the name of Jimmy Brown took up residence in his new home inside the colony, a home considered to be the absolute best in terms of child welfare.

At the age of five, at the end of his nursery education, Jimmy Brown began his transition into a regimented way of life that would stay with him until his teenage years, a way of life he would look back on as being too fearful, too domineering and, not least, too strict. Indeed, the upbringing caused him much pain and anguish.

As for finally leaving the colony's institutional lifestyle as a so-called "confident combatant", when the time came, Jimmy Brown – like so many before him – rejoined society as a naïve misfit. Not only was he completely institutionalised, his years of anxiety and his resulting low self-esteem had become so ingrained that instead of meeting the outside world in a positive frame of mind, he became shy and reclusive.

In 1949, following his release, Jimmy Brown exchanged his loveless surroundings for a new life in the city. The following, his story, is based on real events that took place during the 1950s.

Chapter One

"Not only did we give him a home when no one else would, we adopted him as our very own. And now he wants to throw us out onto the streets?"

A confrontation had arisen as a result of my having 'left the nest'. The squabble with my parents had escalated beyond belief; in fact, it had progressed from the front of the house out onto the pavement.

"You can see what he's doing to us, can't you?"

My mother's tearful pleading with the giant-sized policeman was, in my opinion, a last-ditch attempt to gain the upper hand. Shamelessly, she begged him to intervene. Just how and why the policeman had appeared so quickly, I could only guess... Not that he was on his own; his presence, and the raised voices of my parents, had attracted interest from neighbours and passers-by who – because they had sensed an unfolding family feud – had come to witness a growing public spectacle.

With panic and confusion beginning to set in, plus an inability to cope with the slightest of pressures, I felt myself becoming rooted to the spot. My flushed cheeks to any onlooker must have seemed like a clear indication of my guilt; but blushing was a habit from my childhood days, and something that happened whenever I became the focus of attention.

My rising panic reminded me of an incident that had occurred in my teens. The occasion – an unforgettable one, to say the least – was when, due to a serious misdemeanour having been committed, the entire populace of the children's home I lived in were summonsed to a military-style line-up. Even now as I relived the memory, I could feel a shiver of the emotion that had compelled me to do something bizarre and completely unexplainable.

It was on a Saturday, the one day that every boy and girl in the institution treasured, a day when, devoid of any restrictions and for a few precious hours, each individual could escape into a fantasy world of their own choosing.

"There is a thief amongst us!"

Following that statement, which had impacted like gunfire on the twenty or so boys who were standing to attention, the superintendent spelled out in no uncertain terms the reason for our summons.

"One of you…" The intensity of the officer's gaze became more piercing with every glance. "It has been reported to me that one of you, in the darkness of last night, stole a tasty morsel of food from the home's pantry. If that person steps forward to own up, then the rest of you will be free to enjoy the rest of the day."

Following a few moments of absolute silence and with no response forthcoming, the superintendent gave an ultimatum. "If that's the way you want it, then so be it. You will remain standing here – even if it takes all afternoon. If you want to forego your leisure time, that's your decision."

Questioning looks passed from one boy to the next. I also detected a rising and unbearable tension. Except for the occasional cawing of the nearby woodland crows, it would have been possible to hear a pin drop, such was the overwhelming silence.

The ten minutes or so that had elapsed seemed like an hour of apprehension, and given my susceptibility to any kind of pressure, my face was becoming a beetroot colour. Whether it was this or the fact that I was not reacting convincingly to the stares that were coming from certain individuals, I couldn't be sure. But one thing was certain; in times of trouble, whether I was guilty or not, I almost always caved in – a reaction doubtlessly caused by the prolonged punishments I had endured throughout my childhood.

"It was me!" The pressure finally having got to me, I timidly held up my arm, an act that instantly reduced the tension. It was as if I had waved a wand and all the troubles had gone away.

The irony was, having duly been given a caning, the real culprit was apprehended some days later.

Now, though, pulled back to the reality of the crowded pavement outside our house, the big worry was what I should do next. Due to my inability to stand up to my mother and my ignorance of the law and legal matters, I would no doubt end up taking the easy option; that is, I would submit without so much as a fight.

The battle that was taking place was the culmination of a long-running feud between me and my mother, one that had resulted in my leaving my parents in order to begin a new and independent life. The trouble was, as my relationship with them drew ever closer to its end, the more bitter it became. Now, as far as I was concerned, there was no going back. This was the end of a journey that had begun almost a decade ago in my teens – one in which I had experienced my first taste of family life, and one that could not be retravelled.

The bond with my mother hadn't always been this fragile – far from it in fact. More often than not I had felt deep appreciation for her and her husband for having given me a home and a new start in life. Maybe if I hadn't met a girl who had captured my heart, things might have turned out differently?

Looking at the situation from my mother's point of view, I could see that she didn't want to lose her 25-year-old son, a breadwinner and someone whose presence in the household served as a stabilising factor.

"You should be ashamed of yourself!"

The policeman's stare reduced me to feeling like a criminal, and his pacifying hand on my mother's shoulder was enough to convince me that whatever the outcome, I would forever be judged as being the lowest of the low.

"It's not what you think it is, Sir."

My garbled attempt to offer an explanation to the policeman sounded so feeble that, in a panic, I abandoned it completely.

My thoughts returned to that moment in the solicitor's office when I had applied for a mortgage on a small terraced property I had intended to buy. "It would appear, Mr Seymour, that we cannot proceed with your application owing to the fact that you already have a mortgage on an existing property."

Following a long, long pause in which I had tried to come to terms with what I had just heard, it eventually dawned on me that at some point in my past – possibly around the time of being called up for national service – my father had asked me to add my signature to several official-looking documents. Now, it seemed, not only did I own the house that I had willingly forsaken, I had been misled all along about its ownership.

Following a further discussion with the solicitor, I had been made aware of the legalities of a situation whereby the only option, should I wish to pursue my dream, was to ask my parents to move house – a task that had put the fear of God into me.

However, I still felt puzzled as to why my sister's name hadn't been included as a signatory instead of mine. She was much older and had been employed for a long time; surely she would have been the obvious choice as the main beneficiary?

The stand-off was proving to be a test of wills and although my parents had good cause to involve the neighbourhood policeman, I determinedly – and for the very first time - applied my defiant stubbornness to the situation. What annoyed me most was the fact that the constable had taken sides with my mother - something I despised, considering he was supposed to be a friend of the whole family, including me.

My thoughts suddenly drifted back to a much happier occasion – two or three years ago, I think it was - when this very same policeman had been a witness to a family event that had taken place right here in the very same street and outside the very same semi-detached family home.

Chapter Two

It was the year of 1956. It was an unforgettable year for me and for my 25-year-old sister who, as the recently crowned 'Miss Manchester', was anxiously waiting to embark on what promised to be one of the most momentous days of her life.

"Transport for Sylvia Seymour-Smythe?"

I smiled to myself on hearing that name; it had my mother's influence written all over it. The family surname was Seymour but, as was her habit whenever trying to impress, she always included the name 'Smythe', being an elaborate version of 'Smith', her maiden name before marriage.

The bespectacled and well-dressed gentleman introduced himself as her escort for the day's outing. He sheepishly wiped his shoes on the doormat before adding, "If it's alright with you, I won't come inside; I'll wait by the car."

"I'll only be five minutes," shouted my sister Sylvia from the lounge.

"Don't you mean ten minutes?" My cheeky comment was proof that I was more than familiar with some of my sister's routines - especially the application of make-up in front of the mirror.

My father retched and coughed his way down the stairs – his morning 'clearing of the chest', as he would say – and exclaimed, "Have you seen the car outside the house? It's a Rolls Royce! A big black one, all polished just like new and with a chauffeur with a peaked hat!"

Bypassing my father - the immaculately turned-out head of the household that he was - I pushed the front door open to feast my eyes not only on the Rolls but also on the throng of neighbours who had filled the street with open-mouthed curiosity. In haste, my mother immediately returned to the living-room mirror to inspect her appearance and to add any necessary adjustments, an act that caused her to remove her hat and black veil and replace it with another one.

Announcing his intentions to lead us outside, 'His Lordship' (my sister's favourite nickname for our father) was subjected to the closest scrutiny by his wife. She was determined to present to the outside world the most handsome and best-dressed husband in the world. She gave one final tweak to his tie and breast-pocket handkerchief before handing him his new leather gloves.

Beneath the warm rays of morning sunshine, the four of us finally walked the short distance to the front gates, me carrying what I presumed to be a covered-up bundle of Sylvia's wardrobe. Ahead of me, my proud sister strode arm in arm with her mother and father. As the waiting bystanders cheered their approval at Sylvia's choice of outfit, I felt myself becoming immersed in the same pride as that of my parents.

The well-mannered man opened the car's rear door and George and Mary, my parents, were ushered onto a plush leather bench-seat. Meanwhile, I gazed at a scene that closely resembled a movie spectacle – crowds of onlookers, including a local policeman, all smiling and waving.

Satisfied that my parents were comfortable, our escort turned to me and invited me to sit on the forward-facing back seat, and the chauffeur placed Sylvia's wardrobe in the boot of the car. Finally, having received many messages of good luck from her admiring audience, Sylvia took hold of our escort's outstretched hand and, like a princess, was led smilingly to the opposite side of the gleaming vehicle where she sat down next to me. With one final wave to the street's occupants, plus an instruction to the waiting chauffeur, our escort stepped into the car and closed the door behind him.

As the vehicle's engine purred into life and the crowds shouted their wishes for Miss Manchester's good fortune at the Miss United Kingdom finals, the car and its occupants received a surprise cheer from all the onlookers and a formal salute from our neighbourhood policeman.

"By way of a surprise, I've decided to take you on the scenic route to Blackpool, the one over Belmont."

Acknowledging our escort's announcement with a smile of approval, my father entered into a conversation with him regarding the journey's itinerary. However, for me, the name Belmont brought to mind, with a twinge of excitement, the illuminations and the Blackpool Pleasure Beach.

The unmistakeable smell of leather and the sheen of a well-polished interior was the kind of luxury that suited my mother down to the ground and, judging by the look on her face, she had attained her ultimate goal. Even the face on her fox-fur stole seemed to mirror her smug satisfaction.

Edging myself closer to the window, I got ready to wind it down; I loved fresh air and the atmosphere in the car was already thick with the scent of perfume. As I took note of the sliding glass panel that separated the driver from his passengers, I thought, *Just as well; otherwise our chauffer might have been suffocated.*

I sat back, enjoying the sensation of being 'lord of the manor', and began comparing today's strange and rather artificial circumstances to that of my own life's journey since becoming a member of the Seymour family. It all seemed so surreal.

Reaching for the silver cigarette case in his jacket pocket, His Lordship offered one of his favourite brand, Navy Cut, to the stranger – the person I had rightly or wrongly assumed to be Sylvia's manager. As George struggled to remember the gentleman's name, my sister quickly came to his rescue.

"Bloomberg! His name is Mr Bloomberg."

When Mr Bloomberg explained that he didn't smoke, my father handed a lit cigarette to my sister before settling back in his seat, a performance that immediately prompted me to further wind down my window.

That name… Mr Bloomberg. My humour began to get the better of me as I compared it to my father's favourite expression: "Bloomin' heck", "Bloomin' hell," or "What the bloomin'…" I could just imagine what might be going through my father's mind, and his temptation to make a joke of the name. But under the circumstances and with his dominant wife keeping a watchful eye on him, I realised my concern was unnecessary.

Pondering our escort - a shy and nervous-looking person – I began to form a picture of someone who, by way of making a name for himself, had claimed my sister, 'Miss Manchester', as his special project. On the other hand, maybe I was jumping to conclusions? Sylvia's personal life had always had an aura of mystery and intrigue about it. So maybe Mr Bloomberg, who was sitting next to her, was a personal friend, an acquaintance even, or maybe he was the person who had first initiated the idea of Sylvia becoming eligible for the Miss whatever-it-was title?

The more I pondered, the more I realised that everything about today was far from simple and straightforward. If anything, it was just like that recent newspaper photograph that was presently adorning my bedroom wall – the one captioned 'A Family Success'. In it, the 'Seymour-Smythe' family had been portrayed as a loving and devoted family, one whose togetherness had played a major role in achieving the outcome of a newly elected Miss Manchester.

As I looked at my sister's beautiful reflection in the car window, I tried piecing together what little I knew of her progression to her beauty-queen title, an exercise that drew a complete blank. The only real clue was her regular weekly visitation to the Ritz Ballroom in Manchester, a night-time venue where beauty contestants, amongst others, paraded their charms and good looks. Owing to the demands of work and pursuing my own hobbies, there was little time for conversation in our house other than at the weekends and it was only then - depending on the prevailing mood of my mother – that the details of my sister's vexing personal life was aired. Often confused and embarrassed, especially when voices became raised, I invented excuses to either leave the house or go upstairs to my room. I hated arguments or trouble of any kind – especially when they resulted in my mother's tears.

In an attempt to shut out these unpleasant thoughts, I focussed instead on the more pleasing image of my recent acquisition, a girlfriend who very conveniently lived just two streets away. Wrapped up in my own thoughts, I almost failed to notice the white-sleeved, point-duty policeman who, as our vehicle drew near to a pedestrian crossing, saluted. My mother's reaction – one of immense satisfaction and surprise – convinced me that regardless of how the remainder of the day progressed, nothing could come anywhere close to what had just happened. The look on her face as she leaned back in her seat was one of someone who had just been paid the noblest of compliments. It reminded me of something my sister Sylvia had once told me: "If ever you want to get around Mother for any reason at all, make sure you include the name 'Smythe'; nothing pleases her better."

Chapter Three

"Penny for your thoughts?"

I brushed aside the casual remark from my father as I attempted to divert his attention to the scenery outside, whereupon he began a dialogue with the unfortunate Mr Bloomberg.

With a feeling of relief at having been granted an extension to my musings, I returned to my own dream world. And aided by the hypnotic flashes of sunlight that filtered through the car window, and the motion of the car, I gradually succumbed to my…

***

Today was no ordinary day. It was in fact Saturday – visiting day at the orphanage; a day when just a handful of young children would receive a rare visit from either one or both of their parents and, if in luck, a gift of a tasty morsel.

Quite unexpectedly the name - my name – "Jimmy Brown" had been shouted out during a match of kick-about football and as a result I now found myself perched on the wooden bench outside the orphanage's lodge house.

Dressed in my Sunday clothes and sitting beside a few other boys and girls, I anxiously waited and wondered if either one or both of my sisters would be coming to visit.

Although it was already late summer, the warmth of the sun's rays raised both the temperature and my excitement. Unable to sit still, I monitored the time on the house clock and double-checked that the name 'Jimmy Brown' had been included on the visiting list.

Suddenly a loud honking sound from a car that had stopped outside the tall iron gates prompted an orderly from within the complex to admit the visitors.

Must be someone posh, I thought to myself, observing the gleaming, open-topped vehicle as it did a U-turn outside the superintendent's house. *I wonder who they've come to see?*

As the silver-coloured car finally stopped, an elegantly dressed lady rose from the back seat and called, "Jimmy! It's me, your sister Sylvia!"

Strangely, I didn't recognise her until I got closer to the car and came face-to-face with that unmistakable, warm smile.

It had been months since her last visit. On that occasion she and my other sister Vera had taken me to Wilmslow for the afternoon. Now, looking more grown-up and prettier than ever, I felt very proud of Sylvia, and I noticed the envious stares of my fellow inmates as they stood gawping at the car.

"We're taking you to Alderley Edge for the afternoon," said my sister who, having duly signed the visitor's book, added, "Won't that be nice?"

Inviting me to shake hands with the two front passengers in the car, she said, "This is Mr Seymour and this is Mrs Seymour, my father and mother."

Shyly acknowledging the front-seat couple, I accepted my sister's invitation to climb onto the back seat where, noticing my admiration for the vehicle's beauty, Sylvia added, "In case you didn't know, it's a Sunbeam Talbot!"

However, owing to my institutionalised upbringing and my eleven years in this isolated colony, the name of the vehicle meant nothing to me.

In retrospect, I can't deny that my first impression of Mr and Mrs Seymour was one of complete awe –

so much so that on hearing my sister address her new father as 'His Lordship', I actually presumed, in all ignorance, that the Seymours had royal connections.

Mr Seymour smiled kindly at me before diverting his attention elsewhere. From his polished shoes and grey pinstriped suit with matching breast-pocket handkerchief to what looked like a pair of soft leather driving gloves, he really did give the impression of being a person of wealth and stature. All that was missing was a trilby hat, but from that day to this, I never saw him wear one. Maybe the Vaseline he used to give his hair a shiny, swept-back look added to the effect? Or could it be that in order to please his wife, who judged him to be a Bing Crosby lookalike, he had to maintain a kind of film-star image for her sake?

Not only did Mrs Seymour's appearance stand out, she reminded me of a duchess from one of those black-and-white silent films that we watched in the institution – a person who attracted attention on account of their expensive-looking furs. Those and the lace veil covering her face were sufficient for me to assume that in certain circumstances a curtsy or a bow would not be out of place. Another thing that stood out about Sylvia's mother was her height, which at five feet two inches seemed inadequate for someone of such standing. But despite her husband's superior five feet nine inches, he always reacted smartly to her instructions.

Having convinced myself that my sister could not have found herself a better mother and father, I briefly wondered why it was that the middle-aged Mr and Mrs Seymour hadn't adopted my other sister too, the one who only this year had left the colony? Leaving that and other thoughts behind, I soon began to wallow once again in my own secretive make-believe world, the one where Jimmy Brown lived a carefree life on the other side of those perimeter gates.

As the vehicle sped down the notoriously steep hill and over Twinney Bridge towards Wilmslow, I excitedly remembered the time on a previous visit when Sylvia had bought me a catapult. Selfishly, I wondered if she would buy me another present now.

But when the car did come to a stop, it was outside the Rex Cinema where Sylvia said, "I'm just going to ask what the film will be next month when it's your birthday. Maybe Vera and I could come to see you for the day?"

Much to my sister's delight it would appear that the forthcoming film starred David Niven. For her, the film was the ideal choice; whereas, deep down, all I could think was, *Why couldn't it have been a Western?*

***

"No! Not that way, Jimmy!"

Mrs Seymour disapproved of my attempts to pour myself a cup of tea and relieved me of the china teapot to show me the correct way of holding the vessel. My lack of table etiquette made me wish I was somewhere else. I almost wished I hadn't come. But the timing of the sandwiches and cakes arriving at the table could not have been better. With my guilty conscience now put to one side, I feasted my eyes on the selection of food, especially the cream cakes.

Taking stock of my open-air surroundings at the Wizard Inn, I felt myself being drawn towards the nearby Alderley Edge copper mines, where on numerous occasions I had searched for buried Roman treasure.

"Come on, tuck in! You're a growing lad. Eat as much as you want!"

I shyly accepted Mr Seymour's invitation while at the same time trying to ignore his wife's remarks about the quality of the table linen and other such observations. Never having been in a situation like this before, I was grateful that my sister had discreetly shown me how to use the serviette, an accessory that was new to me.

All too soon the conversation turned towards the return journey to the institution, which although inevitable was a subject I had tried to resist until the very last minute. As always, that inescapable feeling of emptiness tugged at my heart and created a vacuum of churned-up feelings that lasted for days on end.

***

My next encounter with Mr and Mrs Seymour occurred two years later at the age of fifteen when during a stay in a Manchester foster home, I received an invitation to visit them for Sunday-afternoon tea. The weekend of that visit still holds an abundance of memories for me. One memory was boarding a double-decker bus to the centre of Manchester and instead of arriving at the city centre, I found myself in another location altogether. Having heard "Piccadilly!" shouted out by the bus conductor, I had alighted not at my destination but, rather, at The Piccadilly public house, some two miles further on. Fortunately my sister Sylvia had continued to wait outside the city-centre Queen's Hotel where, following my out-of-breath explanation for my delay, we then boarded the Stalybridge-bound bus to where she lived.

The experience of living in a built-up city was still new to me. It was difficult to get used to an atmosphere that was thick with industrial smells and grime rather than a pleasant countryside aroma.

To think that during all those years spent in the institution I had dreamt of nothing else but the special day when my release would become a reality, and now that it had, my everyday life had become an obstacle course – a pathway full of pitfalls where, owing to my immense naivety, one wrong turn and I would easily become a laughing stock.

"We get off at the next stop, Jimmy."

I turned my attention towards the approaching vicinity, one that - compared to the blackened terraced houses at the start of the journey – was a pleasant relief. The bus conductor's proclamation that we had arrived at "Fairfield" was the signal for our departure and as we stepped onto the pavement, my sister pointed towards the next immediate turning to our left – a wide avenue that was flanked by trees and grass verges.

Arriving at what appeared to be a three-storey, mansion-sized house at the top of the street, I was not in the least surprised when Sylvia announced that we had finally arrived at our destination. The size of the garden, with its ornate fencing and well-tended shrubbery, was similar to the immaculately kept gardens at the institution, which I had always deeply admired.

"Mind the steps, Jimmy!"

Following behind my sister, I climbed the five stone-coloured steps to a platform area on which there were placed two stone ornamental plant holders, each containing sweet-smelling flowers.

On opening the front door Sylvia pointed to a stair banister and remarked, "We live on the top floor – three flights up."

Not knowing what to expect next, I climbed the stairs to the top of the house. I remember that my first thoughts were, *How strange; I feel as if I'm back at the home where I grew up.*

Satisfying myself that it was probably the smell of polish on the wooden banister or the green linoleum that was familiar, I at last entered the home of Mr and Mrs Seymour.

"Come on in, Jimmy. Take a seat while Sylvia and I prepare the table."

Following Mrs Seymour's invitation, I gingerly placed myself on the armchair by the fireplace and, assuming it to be of great value, sat in an awkward, straight-backed position. So far, I had failed to feel in the slightest bit relaxed, despite Mrs Seymour's attempts to make me feel at home, and I overwhelmingly wanted to be somewhere where I could feel more at ease.

Being left in the company of Sylvia's father, I realised that at some point I would be expected to engage in some form of conversation, a terrifying task that occurred sooner rather than later.

"What do you think of the house then, young man?"

"It's nice, Sir!" I replied.

"You don't talk much, do you?"

No sooner had he said those words than Sylvia popped her head through the doorway.

"Can't you see he's shy? Why don't you show Jimmy round the garden?"

The next voice was that of Mrs Seymour, informing her husband that he should delay the tour of the grounds on account of tea being imminent.

Whilst appreciating Sylvia's concern for my awkwardness, it by no means helped to diminish my fear of making an exhibition of myself. I had no confidence in my table manners or any other type of etiquette. Fortunately, now sitting by the window, I was able to use the view as a distraction and, not only that, I had just noticed the family pet - a blue-coloured budgerigar in a cage. I had never seen a caged bird before and my excitement at the prospect of it leaving its confinement and perching on my hand was almost too much to bear.

"We'll let it out as soon as the china has been put away. Its name is Joey, but we're not sure whether it's a boy or a girl."

Mrs Seymour's mention of the china tea service not only brought back memories of that day trip to the Alderley Edge café, it also triggered recollections of something she had said whilst examining her cup: "It's not genuine china, you know!" It was becoming obvious, even to me, that, as nice a person as she was, Mrs Seymour was strong-minded and felt a certain superiority to those around her. However, despite this, as the afternoon wore on, I had not only formed a picture of my sister's home life, I had actually visualised myself being a part of it.

***

Accompanied by many memories of the day's visit, I set off on the return journey to my lodgings with a real mix of emotions. I had so many questions that appeared unanswerable and beyond my limited understanding of the world at the time.

"Goodnight, Jimmy."

Engulfed in the lingering aroma of my sister's perfume – a reminder of the past few hours – I became filled with uncertainties about my future.

"I'll be in touch as soon as I can."

Waving goodbye to my sister and her parents, I suddenly became aware of how Sylvia's immaculate appearance and beauty contrasted with the street's terraced house in which I was now living. It was also a stark reminder of how different my lodging place was compared to the fresh air and green fields of my childhood. Not that I wished to go back there! Anything was better than being told constantly what to do or, worse still, being punished. Besides, I had now got a taste for the freedom I had always wished for and now that the shackles had been removed, so to speak, my newfound independence was a matter for celebration – not that I had yet worked out how to celebrate!

One week later I accepted another invitation for afternoon tea, only this time it came from my other sister Vera, who lived in a nearby foster home in a neighbourhood that boasted semi-detached houses and lawns.

Unlike the atmosphere at the Seymour house, where I had been afraid of showing myself up, I felt completely at ease with the foster family I now lived with, a family whose down-to-earth manner made me wish I could have experienced a normal upbringing. In truth, I could not fault the food or care I received from my foster mother but at the same time, I also felt that my presence in the household was more about the financial benefits she received from the town hall towards my upkeep. Perhaps it was my sensitive nature - a relic of my upbringing - that caused me to experience things more acutely; perhaps I was seeing mountains rather than molehills...

It was rewarding to see that my sister Vera had settled with a caring family, a fact made obvious by the way she interacted with them and talked openly about her work and social life. In a way I felt envious of her achievements, but then I reminded myself that she had left the orphanage homes approximately three years before I had, thus allowing her more time to acclimatise to life beyond its gates.

Chapter Four

"How would you like to live with Mr and Mrs Seymour?"

I was taken aback by the Children's Officer's suggestion. I was thrown off balance and, as usual, it was a challenge to overcome my indecisiveness in order to make some kind of commitment.

Acknowledging my meekly spoken "Yes" – a statement fraught with uncertainties – the officer continued, "Your sister Sylvia thinks it would be the best thing for you, and not only that; her parents might consider adopting you."

My confused mind was a minefield of turmoil where ifs and buts piled higher and higher.

The officer then informed me that instead of going to my place of work on the following Monday morning, he himself would be escorting me to my new place of residence with the Seymours.

Following what sounded like a whispered conversation with my present foster mother, a person whom I now began to feel sorry for, he again reminded me of the following Monday appointment, exclaiming, "Make sure you have all your belongings ready!"

***

By the time the Children's Officer arrived on the Monday, I had undergone all the processes of readying myself, including wrapping up my clothes and Bible in a brown-paper parcel. My final wave of goodbye was more of a formality for me, but it contrasted greatly with the sentimentality being displayed by my handkerchief-waving foster mother. Unlike me, she had filled up with emotion.

"Are you pleased to be going to your new home?" asked the officer as we sat on the bus.

"Yes, Sir," I replied.

"We'll be there in an hour's time." Then, following an interval of silence, the town-hall official remarked, "You don't talk much, do you? Is there nothing you can say?"

But how could I join in with any kind of discussion? I didn't know anything about anything that was normal and everyday, so I tended to keep quiet rather than make a fool of myself.

There was one troubling thing occupying my mind too; it was the thought that, having just been enrolled as a bugler with the local 'Church Lads Brigade' band, I would now have to forego the pleasure of owning a bugle and a uniform.

"Haven't you got any hobbies?"

"No, Sir."

What I didn't disclose to him was that I had collected stamps during my time at the institution and that on the day of my release, they had been stolen from me.

"My little boy collects toy cars and he can name every make of car there is."

That proud boast did little to evoke any interest in me. Instead of showing any enthusiasm, I automatically retreated into my silent and secret world, the one that had been my saviour throughout my unhappy childhood.

How can he say things like that? I asked myself. *Surely he must be aware of my background and the fact that I've spent my childhood in a secluded colony, a place where cars and civilisation are only dreams.*

In a final attempt to prise something from my closed lips, the trilby-wearing officer exclaimed, "No more working at the electrical shop, then? You're a very lucky young man! A new home and a new job!"

"Yes, Sir," I replied.

Little did he realise that the school-leaving apprenticeship he had originally found for me had turned out to be disastrous and that instead of learning to be an electrician, I had served my time as a skivvy. This was perhaps not the answer he wanted to hear, so I reverted to my uncommunicative self, hoping that my stubbornness had finally silenced him.

My view of the Children's Officer was a poor one as he had been one of those who had helped to create my low self-esteem. Not only did he display an unsympathetic attitude, I also resented the fact that from day one he had placed me in a working environment that had given me nightmares. Yes, I had told him that becoming an electrician was my preferred choice, but what I hadn't expected was being placed in a small business that specialised in the conversion from gas power to electric, something that was fashionable amongst the local householders. Learning the basics and carrying out all the menial tasks was one thing, but what I hadn't envisaged in my apprenticeship was the requirement to work underground; it was a job that necessitated my threading electrical cables and conduit piping beneath house foundations. It was this kind of work that on one occasion had caused me to become trapped in pitch darkness and, as a result, I suffered a reaction that lasted for days. My eventual rescue caused me to thank God himself. Yet during that terrifying time, I somehow had been able to draw on my childhood habit of escapism to stave off the intense feeling of claustrophobia.

On arriving at our destination, I stepped off the bus outside the so-called Tram Office, which was a small building where bus drivers and bus conductors either swapped shifts or filled up their hot-drinks canisters.

"You've been here before, I believe?"

"Yes, Sir," I replied.

"Well, in that case, I'll let you lead the way."

I couldn't help thinking that he already knew the way and that his remarks were merely a last-minute attempt to be sociable.

Full of apprehension about what lay in store for me at the Seymour house, while at the same time trying to look as inconspicuous as possible, I led the officer to the front of the building and pushed open the gate. There, he immediately resumed control. On arriving on the top step he took off his raincoat and trilby and, having satisfied himself that he was presentable, pressed on the ornate bell push.

On completing the introductions, we negotiated the three sets of stairs - the ones I had remembered - before entering Mrs Seymour's living quarters. Mrs Seymour invited me and the officer to take a seat whilst she warmed the kettle. Yet again that same china tea set, as it lay spread across the white starched tablecloth, became the talking point of the two adults, whereas the only two things that held my interest were the food and the budgerigar.

As soon as my hunger had been satisfied I was invited to go to my bedroom to unpack my clothes and to stay there whilst the Children's Officer and Mrs Seymour completed their paperwork.

"Just to remind you, you're a very lucky young man. Not many children of your age get the opportunity that you've been given. I hope you'll show your gratitude to Mr and Mrs Seymour by behaving in the manner that you were taught."

Those words were the last I would ever receive from any town-hall official. As I closed my bedroom door on the day's events, I couldn't help thinking that I had now begun a new chapter of my life.

***

"Now then, Master James! Since you're known as Jimmy, Jimmy Brown will have to do – at least for the time being. Make yourself at home and if you wish to explore the garden, please do so. Your sister and Mr Seymour won't be home from work until six so if you want a sandwich before then, let me know. In the meantime I have some work to do in the kitchen and by the way, there's a radio in your room if you want to sit and listen to it."

The thought of actually having access to a radio, and being able to turn the knobs myself, was probably the most exciting thing possible but, having already earmarked the garden as being my number-one priority to explore, I decided in favour of the open air.

By the time I had completed my tour I had discovered an array of flowerbeds, a raised vegetable patch and a collection of shrubs. There was also a hedgerow, out of which rose a black and white wooden sign with large lettering that said 'School Clinic'. But my attempts to make any sense of why such a sign should be on display in front of the Seymour residence were forgotten when my curiosity was aroused by the numerous white, marble-like rocks that were scattered about the grounds.

***

"Did you enjoy the garden?"

"Yes, Mm," I replied.

"Do you like gardening?"

For the first time in a long time I was able to say something positive on account of having learned all about gardening whilst at school, so without any hesitation I began divulging my knowledge of the many plants and vegetables I had cultivated over the years.

"You've now got a helper, George. Jimmy knows a lot about gardening, don't you, Jimmy?"

Provoked into conversation, following the evening meal, Mr Seymour replied, "If that's true and you promise to do the gardening for me, I'll treat you to the pictures whenever there's a good film on."

"You're very privileged, Jimmy!" exclaimed Sylvia. "I have to pay when I want to see a film."

Feeling more relaxed, I then offered my dishwashing services, a suggestion that received an immediate response.

"Not today, young man. We wouldn't want to break any china teacups, would we? Why don't you sit in the chair by the hearth and make yourself comfortable? I'm sure your sister would like to know all about what happened today."

Obeying Mrs Seymour's suggestion, I positioned myself next to the budgerigar in the hope that I might be allowed some form of contact with it, a move that attracted the attention of Mr Seymour.

"You can let him out later when we've finished our cigarettes. His name's Joey and he sometimes talks. His favourite words are 'Pretty Joey' or 'Pretty boy'."

Astounded by what he had just said, I impatiently

waited for Sylvia and her father to finish their smoking so that the window could be closed, although judging by their body language it looked like being a very long wait.

***

"Did you sleep well, Jimmy?"

Awaking to the sound of Sylvia's voice the next morning, I not only noticed the rays of early-morning sunshine but detected the mouth-watering smell of toasted bread.

"I'm off to work now. I've filled the teapot and there's some toast on the table. I'll see you tonight."

Waving goodbye to my sister, I couldn't help but think how smartly dressed she looked for someone who was going to work. I already knew she worked for an insurance company, having learned the details of her employment (and that of her father) during last night's conversation. In fact, it was the detailed discussion concerning my future and the kind of family life I was about to inherit that had been the cause of my sleeplessness that night. I had never known such a degree of excitement in my whole life, and having recalled last night's revelations I decided the first thing on today's list would be the exploration of the garage in which Mr Seymour housed his car.

"You can't see the garage," he had said. "It's underneath that raised vegetable patch in the garden. It used to be an air-raid shelter, which is why it was camouflaged to look like a garden."

Inevitably my thoughts reconnected with my childhood and the cold, damp interiors of the institution's so-called 'dugouts'. Even to this day I can still smell the oil lamps as we sat huddled together during the long night-time vigils and my relief on hearing the wail of the all-clear sirens.

As I dressed in readiness for the day ahead, I heard voices on the lower landing. It seemed that Mrs Seymour's business associates had already arrived. She had informed me during last night's conversation that today would be a working day and that my leisure time would pay dividends if it were spent walking round the neighbourhood, so I decided on the warm clothing and the mackintosh that the institution had provided me with as rainclouds had begun to gather.

It all seemed so strange. Here I was eating my toast and jam and drinking tea in the presence of a talking budgerigar and feeling like someone who had had all their wishes come true. I had much to owe to my benefactors, the wealthy and influential Mr and Mrs Seymour.

"Good morning, Jimmy. I'm glad to see you're up and dressed and helping yourself."

For a moment I felt confused by the way in which Mrs Seymour was clothed, so in a bid to deflect my gaze, asked her if I could switch on the radio.

"Of course, help yourself. I've just come up to get some milk. The milkman must be late today."

No sooner had she left to go downstairs than my mind gave way to the most obvious of questions: what had become of the lady-like, immaculately dressed woman of yesterday, and why was she wearing a headscarf and an overall, its pockets bulging with cleaning dusters?

With an inkling of disappointment beginning to take over, I recalled an incident that had taken place on the day of my release from the institution – a day when, for the very first time and without any accompaniment, I had boarded a city-bound double-decker bus. That was the day when my perception of adult women and all that they stood for had turned into a let-down of immense proportions; a day when for the first time in my life I had actually seen a woman - a bus conductress - who not only smoked and acted in a manly fashion, but wore trousers. In a not too dissimilar state of mind, I now experienced that same disillusionment, which took the edge off my newly found sense of prestige.

***

By the time of the family meal on my second day I had come to accept that the grand-looking building in which we lived was in fact a clinic of some kind, whatever that meant, and that Mr and Mrs Seymour were the caretakers – hence our top-floor living quarters.

"But they don't have to pay any rent and the heating is free," concluded Sylvia.

I was also to learn from my sister over the next few days that her mother and father were responsible for the upkeep of the premises, a position that required Mr Seymour to attend to the garden amongst other duties, and Mrs Seymour to be responsible for the cleaning - including the washing and stoning of the outside steps.

***

"You'll be pleased to know that George has found you a job, and that you're to attend an interview next Monday."

This announcement by Mrs Seymour at the

conclusion of the evening meal was an encouraging indication of my changing fortunes. It also signalled a change of attitude, in that she now appeared to have adopted a controlling and parental manner towards me.

"Well, Sylvia, we now have a good excuse for going to town on Saturday. We can't have your brother turning up for work in those clothes. Isn't that right, Jimmy?"

"Yes, Mm," I replied, wondering why the new suit of clothing I had inherited did not appeal to anyone else's tastes. I wondered if I would be required to wear a suit at the city-centre departmental store where my interview was going to be held. Remembering the dark blue overalls from my so-called electrician's apprenticeship and the obnoxious dirt and smells that had clung to them, it was little wonder that I felt grateful to my other sister for detecting my unhappiness and using her influence to improve my circumstances.

By the Friday of my first week I had not only learned the layout of the district and the various routines of my clinic-come-home, I had also experienced my first ever hint of feeling like I actually belonged to a family, something that until now had been one of those childhood dreams that had always led to nowhere.

My attention was drawn by a lady who had just arrived at the front door at the end of the day – a person who, judging by her blue outer garment, was one of the nurses belonging to the medical clinic.

"Hello, James! Will you give this bunch of keys to Mrs Seymour and tell her that I'm leaving my bicycle in the garage?"

Hardly able to contain my excitement at the

thought of a bicycle being left by itself and doing nothing, I delivered the message in the hope that I could find enough courage to ask Mrs Seymour if the bicycle's owner would mind if I rode it.

"I'm sure she won't mind you having a go on it, as long as you take good care and stay near the house. You'll have to wait until Sunday, though."

With that permission ringing loud and clear in my ears, my excitement rose immeasurably and I went to bed feeling that my lifetime dream had come true.

But what if, in my attempts to ride the bike, I fell off and damaged it? Having never ridden a bike before, I knew I would have to be extra cautious. But for as far back as I could remember – probably ten years or so – I had dreamed of the day when such an opportunity might arise and now that it had, little else in the world mattered.

It was whilst thinking about my childhood that I recalled the time when one particular boy in the institution had received a bicycle as a present, a gift that had caused envy amongst all the other children. What became clear to me at this particular moment was why the authorities had made him wait until the time of his release before letting him ride it - a decision, as I saw it, that was more to do with keeping the peace and preventing unsettling jealousies than anything else.

In what was a similar set of circumstances, I remembered the time when my sister Sylvia had bought me an expensive pair of roller skates - the ones that had quality ball bearings in them, or so I was informed – and as a result I was inundated with numerous requests to borrow them. The solution – one that had been decided by the master of the homes – was that I should retain one skate for myself and lend the other to whoever wanted it, a direction that had resulted in my becoming adept in the art of one-legged skating.

***

My Saturday shopping experience in the city centre began firstly with a visit to the Lewis's store where, under the guidance and watchful eyes of Mrs Seymour, I was fitted out from top to bottom with clothing deemed suitable for, as she put it, "a young gentleman".

"Your old clothes will do for working in the garden," she said. "Either that or they can go to the rag-and-bone man."

There was no doubting that Sylvia's mother was now in her element, portraying a doting parent, a lady of substance and someone who, because of her authoritarian manner, demanded respect. Her attire - including her furs, veiled hat and expensive perfume - drew glances of admiration, particularly when in the company of her young and beautiful daughter. Mrs Seymour hadn't been blessed with good looks or even a good figure, but when it came to looking smart and displaying a certain lady-like superiority, which was her trademark, she stood out as being better than anyone else. But it hadn't escaped my observations that my sister Sylvia's good looks drew far more attention, which prompted me to feel extremely proud and important.

Following what seemed like hours of wearily trailing behind the duo, the word "food" suddenly entered into the conversation and with an enthusiasm that highlighted my state of hunger, I eagerly accompanied my escorts to a posh-looking café further along the high street. A waitress wearing a white pinafore apron escorted us to a table and, having given the order for afternoon tea, I was then informed by Mrs Seymour that we were in the prestigious Kardomah Café, this being an up-market coffee house for Manchester business people and such.

Taking great care with my manners, and even more care with the way I held my utensils, I proceeded to devour the delicious cheese-on-toast meal with the conviction that no other food had ever tasted this good.

It was only after I had finished eating that I began to notice the glances directed towards our table, which, as I cottoned on, were all aimed towards where my sister was seated. What I had also noticed was that Sylvia had returned several of them with a smile of acknowledgement and, in one or two instances, even a "Hello".

That same old feeling of being out of my depth had returned to haunt me. Such was my feeling of inadequacy that I turned my thoughts towards the bicycle in the garage, it being, to my way of thinking, my only salvation.

***

Much, much later, having taken leave of the hustle and bustle of the city, we arrived home by taxi to be greeted by Mr Seymour who, following his day's work, had coincidently pulled up in his car at the same time. It was only later when, having finished the evening meal and carried up the parcels from Mr Seymour's car, that I was informed of his business credentials, which, as his wife explained, were those of a high-ranking "grocery" executive, whose status was that of "branch manager".

That, I remember thinking, *is probably the explanation for the amount of food in the pantry*. And it was another reason for assuming that we, as a family, were among the privileged, especially with all the restrictions of food coupons and rationing that were taking place.

With just a couple of hours of daylight left, I finally became seated on the bicycle of my dreams - a lady's bike at that, and one that was obviously an old model. With a few tips from my sister on how to apply the brakes, amongst other things, I nervously set off along the avenue under her watchful gaze where, having become satisfied with my progress, she then continued to the bus stop, en route for her Saturday night out.

With my head in the clouds and my excitement at bursting point, I continued my bicycle riding for the whole of the Sunday until, having been reminded about Monday's work interview, I parted company with it for what I hoped would be only a temporary interlude.

Chapter Five

Two whole weeks had now passed since my interview and already I was beginning to feel as though I had found my destiny, albeit a precarious one in which all types of pitfalls had to be carefully negotiated, especially at my new city workplace – a departmental store. I didn't want my past to be discovered, or the fact that I had had very little experience of life. So rather than risk being accused of being a simpleton - even though that was probably true – I began to cultivate what appeared to others to be an acute shyness. It was probably this front that enabled me to learn and adapt to everyday life and, in so doing, I became rather good at bluffing my way out of awkward situations. There were always going to be occasions when I put my foot in it and, that being said, I was eventually able to thank my lucky stars that I had come through, relatively unscathed.

On the plus side, especially in my private life, and thanks to Sylvia's generosity, I now possessed a second-hand bicycle with a crossbar and front and back lights, something which had not only become a treasured possession, it was one of the reasons behind my improved self-confidence.

With so much change in my personal life and so many opportunities on offer, a dilemma had arisen; I really didn't know what to do next. Indeed, having the freedom to make a decision was so alien to me that it had become an obstacle in itself.

Always detecting my dithering and uncertainty in their early stages, and in a bid to correct me in everything I did, Mrs Seymour exerted her influence in a manner that could only be described as gentle persuasion. As was her way, her dictatorial authority was disguised by a soft voice and a sometimes pleading nature.

One thing that didn't go unnoticed – my sensitive nature had picked up on it straight away – was the undercurrent of friction that existed between Sylvia and her mother, a friction that sometimes erupted – a state of affairs that not only made me upset but caused me on occasions to retreat from the trouble. My fleeing coping mechanism was undoubtedly a legacy of all those years of childhood punishments – not that I had been an habitually naughty boy; it was more the fact that I had been punished for developing a personal and embarrassing affliction that posed regular problems for the authorities and for me. Sunday mornings in particular, I had noticed, were becoming tainted by regular mother-and-daughter squabbling about Sylvia's nocturnal habits over the weekend, something I knew nothing about but something that, judging by the redness and puffiness around Mrs Seymour's eyes, was a matter of growing concern. The only clue, gleaned from the titbits of conversation I overheard, was that Sylvia's choice of men friends seemed to be in opposition to her mother's, a subject on which Mrs Seymour felt entitled to have not only her say but also the last word.

"Are you ready to start the gardening now? It'll give us a good appetite for this afternoon's dinner."

Mr Seymour's timely interruption – his comment bearing all the hallmarks of retreat – was one that I grasped with open arms, especially in view of the tense breakfast-time atmosphere that Sunday.

This was the third time I had dug the garden and weeded out the unwanted growth and because of my hard work and the results that had been achieved, I was promised a cinema treat the following Saturday. As I had already assumed, my trip to the pictures did not include my sister, it being a Saturday night. But what it did include was a Western I hadn't seen before, a cowboy film that had been well publicised.

Having driven across the city in our newly acquired second-hand car - another Sunbeam Talbot but this time with a fixed roof – we were eventually met by the cinema's car-park attendant who, with a salute, guided us into the space he had supposedly reserved for us – a gesture that demanded a suitable tip.

Discarding her travel rug and closing the car door, Mrs Seymour linked arms with her husband in a show of affection that I hadn't witnessed until now. As I followed behind, and for the very first time in my life, I felt what I could only describe as being a sense of belonging.

Brimming over with excitement as the film *Broken Arrow* got under way, my concentration was suddenly distracted by what felt like a hand on my thigh, a warm lingering hand and one that was obviously female.

As if to let me know of her intentions, the girl who was sitting next to me slowly searched beneath the raincoat resting on my knee until finally she located my hand. Then she led it across to where she wanted it, this being the warm crevices beneath her overhanging coat.

The excitement of what was happening not only made my cheeks burn – as I glanced sideways in case I had been observed – I also became conscious of the fact that I was being encouraged to venture into the secret world I had often dreamt of, the one that had tantalised me throughout my teens.

Having guided my hand to the bareness of her thigh she then withdrew her arm as if to invite me to continue, a gesture that included her outstretched leg rubbing against mine. With the freedom that had been accorded me and with the metal suspender clasp having been dealt with, I manoeuvred my hand for the final foray, the one that would lead me to the most inner sanctuary.

Unsurprisingly I had never had any kind of intimate contact with the opposite sex, and considering the great number of boys and girls in the colony where I'd grown up, this was an admission that seemed almost inconceivable. Nevertheless such had been the authorities' strict policies on boy and girl segregation that not only were males and females kept apart, it even resulted in brothers and sisters having to live out their childhoods as complete strangers – a fact that applied to my own circumstances. Only when a family member came to visit did brother and sister become reunited and, more often than not, when this happened, there was a perceived awkwardness about being in the company of the opposite sex.

"What did you think of the film, then?"

Lost in my private, sensual thoughts and with my head still buzzing from all the excitement, I tried my utmost to convince Mr Seymour that it had been the best film I had ever seen. Then as I lay in my bed, attempting to relive my experience, it suddenly occurred to me that the girl's failure to utter any kind of comment or to make eye contact at the film's end was an indication that I had been used... not that I was complaining.

As days turned into weeks and with winter not too distant, I came to the conclusion that I had finally turned a corner in terms of my becoming integrated into the local community, something that Mrs Seymour constantly encouraged. Thanks to her and my sister, I had not only made friends at the local church, I had also become a chorister on account of my childhood experiences with the church choir. This involvement proved invaluable in terms of my growing social life.

Throughout this time, though, there was one dilemma that continued to worry me; at some point in the near future - probably in a few months' time – and because my being adopted had been mentioned, I would have to begin the task of altering my name from James (Jimmy) Brown to James Seymour. My concern was that not only would I have to answer awkward questions concerning my past; there was a risk that I might damage my relationship with my new friends – the ones I had worked hard to establish.

The one good thing about going to work was receiving a wage packet. Although it was destined for the out-held palm of Mrs Seymour each week, it meant that every Saturday I had a decision to make. With my seven shillings and sixpence I could buy a record for Sylvia's music collection or a gift for Mrs Seymour, or I could spend it on making improvements to my bicycle.

Unsure of what the day would bring, I set off across the reservoir route to the second-hand shop on Hyde Road, a place where I had recently purchased a Jussi Björling record for my sister, whose taste in music, apart from the latest rock and roll, included operas and the classics. It was thanks to Sylvia's appreciation of good music that I too now owned Beethoven's 5th *Symphony* along with a Tchaikovsky long-playing record, both of which I listened to whenever my sister loaned me her record player.

"What a lovely surprise!" exclaimed Mrs Seymour as she unwrapped the present I had bought for her. "You know my tastes, don't you?"

Knowing of her love of fine ceramics, I had purchased three second-hand antique china cups and saucers, which now adorned the kitchen table. As she lifted one of them to inspect the maker's details, I prayed that she wouldn't notice the crack in one of the cups. Satisfied that I had made her the proudest woman around, I sat back in my chair to admire what I believed to be a purchase so precious it was bound to rank highly in her collection. What I didn't understand was why, on being washed, they were put to one side and not included in the china cabinet.

One of the things I had noticed about Sylvia's mother was the fact that when everything was going her way, she oozed a natural, flowing charm befitting a high-ranking dignitary – a sure sign that what she had told me about her late father being related to a titled family was probably the truth. The mystery to me was how she came to be married to her partner, Mr Seymour, a person from a totally different background and one who possessed a commonness that his wife looked down on. Her lowly role as a caretaker was even more baffling, although even when dressed in her cleaning uniform, she was still able to demonstrate that sense of detached aloofness whenever the occasion demanded.

"Breeding and manners, Jimmy! If you've got these two ingredients you'll go far in life, and you'll be respected for it."

The 'breeding' part of the sentence was not something I understood but what I did know was that the longer I was in Mrs Seymour's company, the more I became influenced by her teachings on how to become the sort of person she would like me to be. Included in this learning process was her insistence that I should learn to speak properly, just like my sister Sylvia.

"If you're going to accompany me and your sister when we go visiting, we don't just want compliments about your manners; we want a well-spoken young gentleman who will make us all proud. By the way, Jimmy, try doing this to your nose." She cupped her own nose between her thumb and first finger and repeatedly squeezed it in a downward motion, adding, "A Roman nose will make you look more handsome."

For the first time in my life the word 'snob' became added to my personal dictionary, as I tried to accept the peculiar ways of my future mother.

***

The following weekend, after my sister had agreed to forego her Saturday-night social arrangements, the four of us set off for a dinner party that was being given by a farmer and his wife in the hillside district of Glossop, a venue that reminded me of the smallholding next to where I had spent my childhood. Never in my life had I seen such a spread of mouth-watering food on a table and, having been told by the farmer's wife not to be shy, I greedily tucked into all that was on offer, especially the trifle that had an inch-deep layer of fresh cream on the top.

With everyone satisfied and an alcoholic drink having been served, the dinner table then became transformed into a gaming table for card games – something I knew very little of. If it had been a game of dominoes, I would have joined in gladly, but, deciding to watch and learn, I opted to sit by the fire as a spectator. With my cup of tea at hand, a full stomach and the warming embers glowing brightly, I slowly but surely succumbed to the comfort of the homely surroundings and the armchair in which I sat.

Having tried desperately to keep awake for the rest of the evening, I was only too glad when the time came to say goodbye. As we prepared for the long journey home, I wrapped myself in my travel blanket in readiness for the sleep I so desired. Before then, however, and recalling today's outing, I found myself thinking about some of the occurrences that had taken place between the farmer's family and Mr Seymour, which drew my attention to the subject of food rationing. Whilst I was aware of ration books, I concluded that because of Mr Seymour's position as a grocery manager, plus his regular and generous contribution to our own kitchen table, food - or the lack of it – was never a problem for us. And during this evening, an exchange had taken place whereby in return for a large food carton from Mr Seymour, the farmer had made up a present that consisted of a container of fresh cream together with other items of farm produce, including newly laid eggs, fresh vegetables, a cheese and what appeared to be either a leg of lamb or a leg of pork.

***

"Say hello to your mother, Jimmy!"

An unexpected turn of events had resulted in me and Sylvia travelling across Manchester to see my other sister Vera who, in a state of immense pride and excitement, was now encouraging me to shake hands with my real mother.

Turning to the diminutive, grey-haired lady, Vera

added, "This is your son Jimmy. Aren't you proud of him?"

Unsure how to react or what was expected of me, I offered my hand to the stranger who stood before me - an inoffensive and placid-looking lady who, with a smile in her eyes, shyly accepted my half-hearted gesture. I remember she had cold hands and I couldn't help but feel that her faraway look must somehow be connected with her life in the workhouse, an ordeal that was obvious in her demeanour and in the drab way she dressed.

Thinking back to a previous meeting with Vera and her reminiscences about our time in the institution, I recalled the moment when she had told me about an occasion when our mother had been allowed out of the Crumpsall Hospital Workhouse in order to visit us. According to my sister, our mother, along with an accompanying hospital nurse, had sat alongside us on the bench in front of the colony's lodge house, where in a completely relaxed state and with a fixed smile on her face, she had contentedly smoked her cigarettes.

Over a period of time I had learned from Vera that our mother had suffered a bout of depression following the birth of a baby that was stillborn and, as a result, she had been admitted to hospital as a long-term patient. Our father was working full-time and was unable to look after us, so these were the reasons for our eventual admittance to the Manchester-run institution, a countryside colony of some twenty-six homes.

The thought of having yet another mother in my life was confusing, and I decided there and then that I would just leave the matter to work itself out, especially with my mother's fate being the responsibility of the hospital doctors. Another concern for me was not being able to talk about my real mother because of the stigma attached to her being in the workhouse and, even though she was a qualified, full-time seamstress and earning a wage, the tendency of the Seymour family was to avoid any mention of her existence.

Following our afternoon tea and this rare family reunion, the time came for our mother to catch her bus back to Manchester. Her departure caused an intensity of heartfelt emotions, some of which were reflected in the despairing looks of my sisters.

Later that evening and in the privacy of my bedroom, I reflected on our mother's predicament, especially on the sadness of the whole situation, which although not expressed in her face, must have registered with her.

Beethoven's music on the long-player proved to be a distraction. Not only did I turn my thoughts to the girl I had recently met; I also commended myself for having actually found someone who shared both my love of the outdoors and my taste in music. This chance meeting had taken place as a result of my decision to attend a night school where, having been accepted as a pupil at the St John's College of Further Education in Manchester, the chance to fulfil my dreams of learning French and studying music had become a reality.

"You mustn't see her again, Jimmy! Ever! She's much older than you and apart from that, she's a Catholic."

Something that had promised to be a cosy friendship had suddenly been snatched away from me when, four weeks into our relationship and out of the blue, Mrs Seymour vented her disdain at the very thought of my becoming involved with a girl from a different faith. Having eventually submitted to my superior's demands by agreeing not to pursue the relationship, I sulkily set off on my bicycle in the direction of the reservoirs, this being the place where we had last held hands.

"It just isn't fair! Just because we both attend different churches," I muttered to myself.

No matter how I viewed the situation, it still didn't make sense and the more I thought, the more I became angry and frustrated. Inevitably I came to reflect on my own upbringing and, because of the one religion that had been instilled into us, I now found it hard to comprehend the politics of any other form of worship, let alone the shock and horror that Mrs Seymour felt.

Education and learning had always been at the top of my agenda (alongside sports of any kind), which was why, with so many opportunities springing up around me in one form or another, I enrolled at the local theological college, an establishment that was full of books containing all kinds of information. As well as music I now had access to an endless supply of knowledge which, when compared to my limited childhood education, gave me the feeling of having come into an inheritance.

"Your Sylvia was good at English," remarked Mrs Seymour as she picked up a book I had just finished reading. "You know, of course, that she won a scholarship and ended up at the Manchester High School for girls?"

Sylvia's educational achievement was a subject that never failed to inspire me and, as was the case with her mother, I too shared in the same feeling of pride. The strange thing was, however, whenever Sylvia's praises were sung, I more often than not made a bee-line for my private and secretive world, a bolthole where under lock and key and away from anyone else, I guarded to the utmost what had been an unsavoury part of my unhappy childhood. As was the case with my sister Sylvia, I too had attained a scholarship from the colony's senior school but unlike her, I had been prevented from claiming my place in a city school owing to an affliction, something that was labelled 'weak bladder syndrome'. Due to that circumstance and the stigma attached to it, not only did I have to forego a high-school education, I also – because of the embarrassment – became burdened with resentment towards the system I had lived under.

***

It was the summer holidays of a year I would never forget. I waited anxiously for news of my new school, and I felt a huge excitement building in me, knowing that I was nearing the end of an era. But something wasn't right; I could feel it! That was the thought that crossed my mind as the holiday neared its end.

Surely, I thought, *I should have been called to the Superintendant's office by now, in order to be kitted out and to be informed of where I'm going to live…*

Following my return to school for the new term, with not a single word having been spoken, I felt apprehensive about my first day and my spirits were at a low ebb. But the news, when finally revealed, caused me to withdraw further into my unhappy state of mind, inducing a feeling of numbness in me. I knew I was being given excuses.

"Unfortunately, Brown, your marks were wrongly given. As a result, you'll remain at this school until school-leaving age."

Ironically, a few months after that incident I was declared cured of my impediment, but by that time it was too late to alter the arrangements for my remaining school years. I felt that not only had I been robbed and lied to by those in charge; I had had to endure an existence in a place where I was convinced I shouldn't have been.

Much, much later in the darkness and privacy of my bedroom, my thoughts turned towards the sorrowful days of my childhood. It had been a hostile chapter of my life. Even five years later, I found the memories haunting.

I vaguely remembered being promoted from a nursery home to a grown-ups' home at the age of five, where, along with the resident house mother, I became a member of a family unit of twenty-five boys, each of us aged between five and twelve. It was, I think, sometime around my sixth birthday when I first felt the force of a grown-up's slipper on my backside – a punishment for the effects of my weak-bladder ailment. That and subsequent 'good hidings' occurred on a regular basis. These beatings also fuelled a resentment which, added to my previous mental scars, was the reason behind my continuous state of anxiety and low self-esteem.

Out of all of those chastisements, there were two in particular that had been responsible for my decision to run away – but having reminded myself that most, if not all, runaways rarely got very far, I eventually convinced myself that the deed would have to wait until I had given it more thought.

Both of those particular punishments had been administered by an assistant house mother, a stand-in, and it was she - an unusually tall person with a hooked nose – who, having taken control of the home, decided to take matters into her own hands. Choosing a weekday morning and a time when all the school children were walking to the assembly parade ground, she loaded my bed linen onto the top of my head and ordered me to hold it there whilst walking to the laundry building, knowing full well that in taking that route, not only would I clash with my school colleagues, I would also have to endure the resulting stares and comments. If, as on previous occasions, I had managed to walk with my head and eyes facing downwards in order to avoid the embarrassing stares, it would not have been so bad, but in this case I had been instructed to walk upright and in full view.

Not many weeks after that incident and with a stubborn disregard for the consequences, I took it upon myself to verbally retaliate to one of her commands, an act that, apart from shocking her into a state of disbelief, prompted me to regret having been so stupid. Taking off one of her shoes as she manoeuvred me into a corner, she promptly and ferociously laid into me, so much so that I was forced into shielding myself from what felt like a continuous onslaught. Having surprised myself at my lack of tears, I eventually emerged from the attack with the same attitude of defiance and, even though I ached from all the physical hurt, I felt elated at the fact that the house mother had exhausted herself.

How or when my bruises were discovered I cannot recall, but a few days later I was summoned by the ruling superintendent and matron of the homes who, on inspecting my black-and-blue torso, gave the order for me to report to the hospital.

As for the house mother, I never saw her again; it was as if she had disappeared from the face of the earth.

Chapter Six

After sixteen years and ten months, Jimmy Brown ceased to be; instead, he became James Seymour. The adoption ceremony at the town hall was a quick and formal affair, one that, once the signatures had been exchanged, prompted a celebratory lunch at a nearby restaurant.

If I was supposed to feel different, I didn't, but what was more important was the fact that I now had the opportunity to be me – a person with a proper identity and a family and, even more significantly, a chance to break away from my past.

"How would you like to go to London, Jimmy?"

My mother's use of the name 'Jimmy' was thanks to my sister Sylvia and, although she would have preferred the more appealing 'James', it was to remain that way apart from those times when she wanted to impress.

"We're planning a trip to see the Christmas lights on Regent Street and Oxford Street, and we're going to stay at that lovely hotel by Piccadilly Circus."

Having given my wholehearted approval, I embarked on a guessing game regarding the 'circus' part of the statement, but assuming it was something I should get excited about, I began a countdown to the day of our departure.

Having cleaned and polished the car for the weekend getaway – a task that had earned the approval of both my parents – I sat back to enjoy what to me was a 'first' in my experience – a family holiday. I was especially excited to learn of their intention to include a visit to Windsor Castle on the way back.

In spite of my enthusiasm I couldn't avoid the obvious fact that there was an empty seat in the vehicle where my sister should have been, something I put down to her and her mother having fallen out again. The strange thing was, I hadn't sensed any atmosphere whatsoever this time, or, come to think of it, any puffing beneath my mother's eyes – a sure indicator of their on-and-off conflict. Or could it be that she was using her face-net as a cover in order to put on a brave face for me and her husband?

Soon the scenery distracted my thoughts from my absent sister and I brought to mind one of my sister's closest friends – one who lived in the same avenue and whose boyfriend was an American serviceman. Only recently there had been an occasion when Sylvia and she had gone for a ride in the back of the soldier's car, a vehicle I remember vividly owing to the fact that I had never seen another one like it. The name Chrysler stood out as being new to me, but the effect of the shiny chrome bumpers and grills, along with its sleek shape and size, made it a car I would never, ever forget.

The sad fact was that as I was completely occupied with full-time work and my hobbies and I rarely had the time to become involved in Sylvia's pastimes, not that they would have interested me. Hers was a sophisticated world that reeked of expensive perfumes, nylon stockings and clothes befitting a well-to-do lady, most of which had been tailor-made and paid for by her mother.

Although tempted to join in the front-seat chit-chat regarding today's route, I instead focussed on another incident – my mother's telephone conversation at the time of making the hotel reservation. Having communicated the necessary details and requirements for the holiday weekend, she had then signed off as 'Mrs Seymour-Smythe', the same name I had heard mentioned previously. As if to prove a point and having backtracked to Sylvia's attire, I switched my attention to a recent incident in which my mother and her personal tailor had held a discussion regarding the suitability of a certain type of fabric. As a result, the tailor had then made a telephone call to his factory in Leeds and, with the charm of someone who knew how to pamper his clients, had started off by saying, "I'm at the Seymour-Smythe residence."

By the time he had finished his conversation it became evident that he, like others before him, had fallen hook, line and sinker for my mother's convincing play-acting and, as a result, he was a subject ready to do Her Highness's bidding.

Since my mother was not a good traveller it came as a huge relief when the car finally halted at its London destination where, having taken a few moments to acclimatise herself and point out the Lyons Corner House, a favourite of hers, she politely ordered her husband to summon a hotel porter.

Once in the Regent Palace Hotel foyer and during an interval when my father was trying to organise a parking place, I finally came face to face with the kind of pomp and ceremony I had heard my mother describe, and whilst I myself had begun to feel totally out of my depth, Mrs Seymour brimmed with self-satisfaction. Reacting to all the curtsies as if she was used to such attention, inspired her confidence; it was as if she had become revitalised by the hotel's atmosphere, which was deemed perfect in every way.

In what was an attempt to prove my maturity during our evening meal - an incident I'd rather forget - I called to the hotel waiter in order to request an item from the oversized menu with a French-sounding name. What followed was a roar of laughter from both the waiter and my parents. I tried to join in with their merriment while secretly analysing the situation with great embarrassment. Were they laughing at me or at my pronunciation? Or could it be that my child-like naivety had become exposed? Having realised that this was probably the case, I sulkily decided in favour of holding back from any further conversation, a decision that not only allowed me to think things through but led me to withdraw into my own private and comfortable world.

If it hadn't been for my mother's intuition, my tight-lipped stance would probably have continued throughout the rest of the meal; but in a moment of compassion she went to great lengths to explain the wording of the 'a-la-carte' menu, and she instructed me on the way certain words were pronounced.

***

I was amazed at everything I had seen during my London holiday, including Buckingham Palace, Nelson's Column, the changing of the guard and much, much more. However, it wasn't until I arrived at Windsor Castle that my excitement really took hold, especially at the sight of the infamous tower and the Crown Jewels, although, quite unexpectedly, it was the sight of the castle's ravens and the history behind them that gave me the most satisfaction.

My sister's absence continued to remain a puzzle for quite some time and although absorbed with all of my hobbies at home, there were moments when I questioned her reasons for unexpectedly going into a so-called 'rest home', especially with Christmas being not too far off.

In the absence of any explanation, it dawned on me that there might be something wrong with her, a worry that increased every time my mother engaged in upsetting telephone conversations.

My surprise and delight on returning home from work one day to find my sister sitting on the settee wearing a dressing gown was heart-warming. I immediately made a promise to myself that I would try to make up for her long absence and, due to our relationship not being as close as it should have been, I would try to bond with her more.

During the days that followed and because I had noticed a sadness about her, I made the decision to withdraw some money from a savings account and spend it on a bunch of flowers for her – a gift I knew she would appreciate. When she thanked me for my thoughtfulness with a beautiful and disarming smile, I noticed her mood lift; it seemed to be a sign that her health in general was improving. What I couldn't work out – bearing in mind the hard shell behind which Sylvia hid her feelings - was why, at that moment of showing her gratitude and for the very first time in my life, I witnessed glistening teardrops on her cheeks.

The conflict that existed between my sister and her mother - a state of affairs that blew hot and cold depending on the severity of the cause – usually caused me to shy away. I hated bad atmospheres and the long-lasting upset that affected them both. That there was a decline in their relationship was obvious, a fact highlighted by the strange attitude that Sylvia had recently adopted – a kind of deep-down resentment, possibly reflecting something much more disturbing.

If it hadn't been for a driving lesson with one of my father's colleagues, I would probably have never known the facts surrounding Sylvia's debilitating illness but, having mentioned the subject, including her stay at the Timperley care home, I was taken aback by what I learned. Trying not to show my surprise - especially when it came to him offering his sympathies – I completed the lesson despite my concentration having lost some of its edge. I was annoyed that I had been kept in the dark. It also dawned on me that I had been lied to all along. With an innocence befitting a young juvenile and a show of sympathy towards my sister, I actually imagined a tug-of-war taking place between Sylvia and the hospital matron, especially when the moment arrived for her new-born baby to be taken away from her.

To think that she had been pregnant all that time and I hadn't known anything about it! Reflecting on her misdemeanour made me realise how out of my depth I was when it came to the subject of mothers, babies and the opposite sex; in fact, I concluded that I was better off not knowing and that it should preferably stay that way.

Now that I had put two and two together, including the strained atmosphere, it crossed my mind that my sister's future - in terms of her personal life - would be subjected to much more of her mother's interference, and this would inevitably cause Sylvia much concern. For some reason the word 'control' came to mind and the more I thought about it, the more I realised how much of a hold my mother had over her daughter.

Poor Sylvia, I thought.

As had become my habit whenever there were tensions in the home, I would prepare a sandwich and a flask and then set off on my bicycle, a journey that usually took me along pleasant country lanes and through peaceful pastures. Unfortunately, with it being wintertime and snowy now, my bicycle riding had all but ceased. However, in seeking out an alternative I had discovered a new outdoor pursuit, and one that proved to be far more exciting. The only downside was the travelling involved but once the train had arrived at the Peak District terminus, I was rewarded with a landscape that was as appealing as it was challenging. Complete with warm clothing, including a pair of hiking boots, I then set off on an upward climb towards my destination, a hilltop route known locally as Kinder Scout. My long-time ambition was to discover ancient burial mounds; I craved anything to do with exploration and, not wishing to miss a single opportunity, I now focussed my attentions on the beckoning rock formations that lay ahead.

Unbelievably, as I arrived at my first peak it wasn't the geography, astounding as it was, that caught my attention; it was the realisation that amidst this landscape of snow and ice, in this January winterland, I was actually experiencing what felt like a midsummer's sun on my face.

Having decided on a suitable place in which to have my refreshment, I sat opposite a frozen waterfall where, under a blue sky and surrounded by mountain peaks, I became overcome by the sheer beauty of everything around me. With every intake of pure air came a sense of being at one with nature, a kind of spiritual awakening the likes of which I had often read about in biblical stories.

By the end of the day and having been inspired by all I had seen, my infatuation with mountaineering was complete, so much so that my attention was drawn to a comment made by a work colleague who, on describing his walks in the Italian Dolomites, had exclaimed, "It was like being on top of the world!"

Whether or not it was down to my mountaintop inspiration or the recent cinema-film viewing of an overseas missionary's life story, I wasn't sure, but because of what I had experienced that day, I became convinced that my future was going to be in the ministry and in a far-off foreign land. Explaining what I perceived to be my new-found vocation to my mother was one thing, but choosing the right moment became something of a dilemma. However, eventually I took the plunge.

Following a moment of thought and a facial expression that was non-committal, she eventually replied, "You haven't the faintest idea, have you, Jimmy? They, the ministers, get paid a pittance. Haven't you heard the expression 'as poor as a church vicar'? Most of the church ministers come from well-off families and that's the only way they can survive. In the old days and if the family consisted of three sons, it would be a case of one of them being enrolled in the forces, one in politics and law, and the remaining one joining the Church."

Realising that my dream had all but vanished, I retreated to my bedroom in order to sulk, a reaction that was consistent with the level of disappointment I felt.

"Can I come in, Jimmy?"

Feeling the need to pacify me, my mother asked if I would like to see a show at the Opera House, to which, in view of the olive branch she was now offering, I replied "Yes".

Sometime later and having acknowledged that I

would have to continue with my job at the departmental store, I felt uplifted by the sudden thought of my approaching national service obligations which would commence in a few months' time, a requirement that could in fact provide all the foreign travel I craved.

With two or three months having passed since that all-important decision concerning my future vocation, I had not only won a trophy with the football team I played for, my attentions had also been drawn towards the opposite sex, a fact that was beginning to make me wonder whether or not I had been too hasty with my earlier career decision.

There were many female members of the operatic society but due to my feelings of inferiority and inequality, I lacked the confidence to make the necessary approaches required of me. But as luck would have it, an opportunity arose by way of a coach trip to Derbyshire – a five-day stay at a hostel, including a visit to the famed Chatsworth House.

Surely, I surmised, *if there's ever going to be a chance to get to know someone then this is it.*

Arriving in high spirits at our destination and being away from my mother's influences, I literally fell into the supportive arms of a beautiful young girl, an angel - or so I thought - who, in catching me as I stumbled from the vehicle's steps, had provided the perfect excuse for our introduction. Following an exchange of names and a promise to meet up after the evening meal, I proceeded to the hostel's living quarters, mesmerised by the unusually strong feelings that were arising in me.

During the course of the evening I was to learn that my new friend Jenny was a local resident, who, having recently passed her exams at the nearby all-girls' school, was contemplating a career in music, something that had been an interest of mine for most of my life.

From the time of going to bed on that first night I couldn't get Jenny out of my mind. She was, in my opinion, the sweetest, most attractive girl I had ever met - not that I had met many - and already I was telling myself that she was the one I had been hoping for all along.

Not only was the following day's countryside ramble blessed with sunshine and sweet-smelling meadows, but an opportunity arose for Jenny to somehow join her hand in mine and, from that moment until the midday refreshments, I was overpowered by her closeness and the feeling that our fates were being guided towards something special.

Our first kiss - the one I had been anticipating and looking forward to – was mistimed and it caused my face to redden with guilt on account of it taking place in daylight and in front of our colleagues. Unfortunately, with Jenny having taken the initiative, she had unwittingly undone my master plan, the one in which I had intended us both being alone and in the dark prior to making my move. The next kiss, however – one that spoke volumes in terms of our shared passion – not only washed away the embarrassment of the first attempt, it helped to confirm my belief that I had at last achieved the kind of luck I had always longed for. By no means was I the best-looking, the tallest or the brightest, and yet here I was enjoying the attentions of, in my opinion, one of the prettiest girls of the whole group.

Over the course of the next two days and due to our close contact during our walking, swimming and other social pursuits, I began to experience a kind of togetherness that seemed alien to my normal thinking, something I interpreted as being love. It was the first time in my life that I had experienced such feelings... although, with the kind of life I had lived, one devoid of any form of love whatsoever, how was I to know what I was feeling? But what was certain was the fact that tomorrow was going to be our last day together, something that was already preying on my mind.

In the early-morning sunshine, on what promised to be another beautiful day, the whole contingent set off by coach for the eagerly awaited Chatsworth experience, a setting - we had been informed - of such beauty and charm that none of us could fail to be impressed. The quiet mood of Jenny and I as we held hands was in many ways a reflection of the vast open countryside, the one now beckoning from outside our coach's window pane. In it I sensed a tranquillity and isolation that would have appealed to either one of us, a kind of sanctuary for young-at-heart lovers.

My tendency to think too much was a throwback to my childhood days in which, for my so-called lack of attention, I had often been reprimanded. And whilst recalling my young life in the institution, I brought to mind an expression that had been tagged on me for as long as I could remember: 'Jimmy Wish-Wish'. Smilingly, I remembered the many times the house mother had addressed me by that nickname, it being a reference to my continual habit of wishing for everything and anything that would change my life around.

In my determination to make a lasting impression on Jenny, I decided to try out my growing sense of confidence and, with a move that was aimed at breaking the silence between us, I leaned towards her in readiness to plant the most meaningful of kisses on her lips. With a reaction implying that she had already anticipated my intentions, she not only readied herself, she pulled me forward in order to demonstrate her own feelings - ones that were becoming more and more intense.

Arriving at the location in what could only be described as a state of heavenly contentment, my eyes were suddenly drawn to what looked like a palace, a building so breathtaking and beautiful that I found myself comparing it to one of those fairy-tale castles in a children's book, the ones that caused your imagination to run wild.

It wasn't long before Jenny and I both experienced the spellbinding magnetism that Chatsworth was famed for and as we took our first steps towards the building, I felt a tingling sensation that I interpreted as being part and parcel of the love that was building inside me.

No sooner had the tour of the house begun than Jenny pulled me back, explaining, "We don't have to stay with the main party. Let's keep in the background and follow them on our own."

From that moment on, and out of sight of prying eyes, every hidden space became an excuse for our show of affection, being kiss after kiss after kiss. Not surprisingly, at the conclusion of the stately-home tour, we then recuperated by way of breathing in the outside air, being a respite, as it were, from all our activities.

It wasn't long before my feelings took on a change of direction and with my eyes firmly focussed on the water fountain in the distance, I again marvelled at the sheer magnificence of the landscape before me. Having rejoined our group we descended the ornamental steps leading onto the lawns and began our picnic of sandwiches and lemonade.

What I found so fascinating about the relationship between Jenny and I was our ability to read each other's minds, a fact that had become more obvious with every passing day. With that in mind, and knowing today would be our last, I tried to guess what had caused Jenny to suddenly turn away from me. Then I noticed tears on her cheeks and I pulled her towards me. With no explanation being forthcoming and with a faraway look accompanying her silence, I began to wonder if Jenny's tears were the result of something I had said or done, and with an eagerness to put things right, I begged her to tell me the reason.

Her answer was to place her finger across my lips. "You wouldn't understand," she said. "I don't even know myself."

Baffled and confused though I was, I couldn't help but compare the situation to that of my mother and sister; when faced with a similar conundrum they too had classified me as being unable to fathom things out. Happily the mood slowly changed back to how it had been before and, as a result, not only did our togetherness climb to a higher level, it seemed for all the world that our hearts and minds had become one.

As I stepped onto the bus for the return journey I suddenly thought of tomorrow's departure to Manchester, a fact I not only dreaded but one I tried desperately to push to the back of my mind, at least for the time being. For the present, there was an evening's programme of entertainment to look forward to – a Puccini concert performed by the local operatic society as a farewell offering to their fellow music lovers.

The atmosphere inside the school hall was, to say

the least, a happy one, and as I looked around at the now familiar faces I became aware of just how many of my colleagues had formed their own attachments. With this in mind and having acknowledged the extent of Jenny's preparations in making herself even more attractive, I squeezed her hand as a way of letting her know just how special our love was.

Out of all the musical offerings that were performed that evening, one in particular stood out as being one of the most moving pieces of music I had ever heard; it was the 'One fine day' aria from *Madame Butterfly*. It had caused my emotions to almost get the better of me. Fortunately I had been able to stay in control of myself but what I did come to realise was just how strongly one could be affected by music and atmosphere.

At last it was time for the hot-pot supper in the adjoining room, a meal which, in view of our imminent parting, I had already likened to the biblical Last Supper. As there were strong links between the hostel and the local church, it came as no surprise when the minister suggested a hymn-singing session as a way of celebrating the success of the week's get-together. "Especially," he added, "since we are blessed with such an array of choristers."

With the prospect of more time in Jenny's company, I enthusiastically joined the torch-lit procession to the chapel, where having been guided to a position near to the front aisle, I became seated as closely as possible next to my one and only. No sooner had the organ sounded its musical introduction than the whole room came to life, an indication of the audience's appreciation for having been awarded this one last chance of a joyful get-together. Strange as it may seem and knowing that I was as close to Jenny as was possible, I became overwhelmed by a sudden surge of happiness – a tingling experience that I interpreted as being the culmination of so much love and joy within these four walls. Then, all of a sudden and from out of nowhere, I felt an inexplicable trembling in my voice, a kind of stuttering that made it hard to get my words out properly. Persisting with my efforts to join in with what was a very moving piece of music, it suddenly dawned on me that I was beginning to lose control of myself, a fact that became obvious the more I attempted singing 'The day thou gavest, Lord, is ended'. How or why it happened I couldn't explain but tears, the likes of which I hadn't known since childhood, began rolling down my cheeks with a momentum that was both startling and upsetting, and the more I wiped the salt-tasting drops from my lips, the more I realised I was fighting a losing battle.

Aware of my distress and showing a lot more composure than I, Jenny linked arms with me and in a quiet voice said, "It's alright. I understand."

No sooner had her sympathy taken hold, and unable to contain my emotions any longer, I burst out crying like a hurt child, a display that caused me to feel so embarrassed that I parted company with Jenny and hurried into an adjoining room.

On seeing a chair in what looked to be a kitchenette, I sat down to continue with my crying, aware that not only could I not stop, I actually felt as if I was no longer in command of my emotions.

A few more minutes must have passed before the deluge gave way to a more manageable sniffing and as it did so, I felt a strange emptiness, one that was accompanied by a feeling of great relief.

"My goodness me! You could have filled a bucket

with all those tears!"

Astounded that I had been observed, I looked up to find a lady standing near me. She was holding a white handkerchief that she had taken from her handbag. As I took hold of it, I immediately became aware of the fact that not only was she black, she was wearing a hat that was adorned with the most beautifully coloured flowers and wearing a gleaming white apron over her Sunday best.

As a result of this unexpected sight, I slowly but surely began to pull myself together whilst at the same time feeling as if I had been found out.

"It's good for people to cry," she went on. "You should do it more often."

Before handing back her handkerchief, and having digested her comment, I thought back to the last time I had shed tears. It had been a sad moment; at eleven years of age I had been informed of my father's death. "I don't know why you're crying; you hardly knew your father!" It was that sentence, spoken by the house mother, that was to ensure I would never, ever forget the occasion.

"You can keep the handkerchief as a memento but next time, don't hold onto your feelings; let them all out," said the kindly woman in the flowery hat.

By the time I had become reunited with my somewhat bemused girlfriend, I had come to understand some of the reasons behind my outburst and whilst still unsure of its true meaning, I sensed it had been a great deal more to do with my past than my love for Jenny.

Chapter Seven

The letter I had been anticipating all year finally arrived and as I digested the information inside my national service call-up papers, I learned of the details relating to my two-year posting - a soldier's life in one of Lancashire's famous regiments. In a year that had seen the death of the King and the beginning of Queen Elizabeth the Second's reign - not to mention my having fallen in love – yet another exciting prospect had suddenly been added to my list of future ambitions – that of foreign travel.

Surely, I thought, *every regiment goes overseas at some stage?*

From the look on my mother's face I sensed her feelings of displeasure and this made me feel guilty at having to leave home, especially considering the present rift between her and my sister.

"George would have been in the war if it hadn't been for having two left feet!" In her attempt to come to terms with the situation she had brought up her husband's involvement in wartime Britain, adding, "Sometimes his air-raid warden duties kept him out nights on end."

Following a final scrutiny of my call-up papers, my mother said, "You and I will have to have a little talk before your big day comes. You may think you know everything, Jimmy, but believe me, you've got a big shock coming."

My day of departure finally arrived and with it came many words of advice from my parents, including, "Stay out of any trouble. Do as you're told and be on your best behaviour at all times. Just remember the way you've been brought up!" Excited as I was, my only regret was that the army barracks were too near to home, a fact that made me feel somewhat disheartened.

***

"Did you know that you have a hearing problem in your left ear? I'll make an appointment for you at the infirmary."

In view of the fact that I had considered myself to be 'A1' in all matters physical, I not only showed surprise at the army medical examiner's diagnosis, I tried telling myself that since I'd never had a problem he must be mistaken.

It was only after the specialist's confirmation and an in-depth searching for clues that the answer dawned on me and caused yet more hatred of my past life. I relived the many times I had been boxed about the ears, and especially one particular occasion when I had reached the age of thirteen. The day in question had been a Saturday when, in the company of a close pal, I jokingly shouted out, "Cor blimey!" – it being a phrase I had heard on the radio the night before. No sooner had the words left my mouth than I felt the full force of someone's hand across my ear. It was a clout that left me with a ringing sensation in my head and caused me to feel hatred towards my aggressor.

"That's for taking the Lord's name in vain. The next time I hear you say 'God blind me', it will be the cane."

Sometime later, having gradually recovered from a deflated sense of wellbeing, I automatically set my thoughts in motion for my well-rehearsed escape plan, the one that forever tantalised me. But would I ever find enough courage?

***

Thankfully my hearing deficiency was all that was found to be wrong with me and it in no way interfered with my ambitions; a fact confirmed when I appeared before a panel of army careers officers.

"Have you considered becoming an officer? We could put you down for an officer cadre course once you've completed your basic training?"

Not only did I give a definite "no" to the thought of taking command of a platoon and having significant responsibilities, I wondered why it was that the question had even arisen. It was only after some thought that I later realised that they had taken into consideration the fact that I had told them about my having recently read the G K Chesterton book, *On War and Peace*.

Fortunately my writing and reading skills proved to be my saviour when, after completing ten weeks of intensive training, I received a posting to a regimental clerk's school in the South of England, which, following a successful period of training, I graduated from as a shorthand typist and pay clerk.

The reward for my success - a week of home leave – became an opportunity to show off my achievements to my friends and family, and it allowed me enough time to consider my future prospects and the possibility of a posting abroad. Not having dared to tell my mother what my plans were, I returned to the barracks to take up my duties as regimental clerk, a position that, apart from putting more money in my pay packet, provided access to the regiment's hierarchy.

Having settled into my desk job, I soon learned the

ins and outs of regimental procedures and as a result I was able to discover the details of a forthcoming overseas posting, one in which a whole battalion would be setting sail for a tour in Malaysia. Not wishing to miss this golden opportunity I immediately wrote a carefully worded letter to the commanding officer, one in which I expressed my desire to serve abroad.

"I'm very sorry to have to tell you, Private Seymour, your application has been turned down on account of domestic issues. It appears that your mother is suffering from poor health and she's requested that you receive a 'home' posting in order to be on hand whenever she needs you."

Saluting the officer as I left his office, I proceeded to march across the parade ground in a state of pent-up anger, all of it directed at my mother and her attempts to keep me in her sights. In this way she had put paid to my ambitions to travel.

Just one week later whilst typing the details of the forthcoming overseas draft, it came to my attention that a qualified clerk was required at the overseas HQ and not wanting to miss my one last chance, I requested an interview with the captain of our unit.

The result of my having told a few home truths, and explained some untruths too, proved so successful that not only was my wish granted, I had to restrain myself from celebrating out loud my great achievement. But it was only later, when joining up with my pals, that I really experienced the excitement of having fulfilled my dreams – although, bearing in mind the capabilities of my mother, I realised I shouldn't get too carried away until the actual day of my departure. Before then, however, there was a fitness course to be passed – one that required a few weeks of intensive training in the Welsh Valleys prior to embarkation.

***

Finally, and now having completed my training, the moment arrived for me to say goodbye to my family and friends, an occasion that was seized upon by my mother as she began lecturing me about the pitfalls of army life abroad.

"And by the way, your signature's required on this form I've filled out."

Begrudgingly I signed my name on a document that gave permission for my mother to claim half of my weekly army pay – an arrangement she had previously talked me in to. On that occasion she had gone to great lengths to point out that that was what soldiers did, especially when they had family and wanted to help their parents in the upkeep of the family home.

"Who's this Mai Jones, the person who's sent you that parcel?"

The home-baked birthday cake that emerged from the wrapping paper not only surprised me, it caused my mother to react in her usual disdainful manner.

Then she proclaimed, "You shouldn't go around breaking girls' hearts. It's not fair on them. You'll have to thank her for the cake and then tell her you won't be seeing her again."

With the taste of the fruit cake still lingering in my mouth and having finally found some privacy, I recalled my recent encounter in the Welsh hillsides, especially the time when I had plucked up the courage to ask a shy-looking girl for a dance.

The Saturday-night dance at the local town hall

proved to be a pleasant escape from the week's rigorous training. It was also the only place for miles around that provided any form of entertainment and, more importantly, a chance to catch up with civilisation. Never having been associated with anything Welsh in my life, I became captivated by her accent and the name 'Mai', as she pronounced it to me, conjured up a romanticism that was truly exciting.

Our shyness with each other was finally broken under the night sky when, as I walked her to her house, our lips met in what was a tumultuous show of love and passion. It felt like a natural togetherness.

Following a further two weeks of jungle-warfare training in readiness for Malaya, I had achieved the fitness of an athlete. I had also romanticised so much about Mai that I could hardly wait for our next Saturday-night reunion.

"Would you like to stay the night at our house?"

As Mai's surprise invitation took hold, my excitement began to get the better of me.

"I've asked my mother and she said it will be alright as long as you're willing to share the bedroom with my two brothers."

With the necessary permission having been obtained to stay overnight and our last dance together now a memory, I purposely slowed down our walk to her house in order to gain as many kisses as was possible, knowing from what she had told me that I would be faced with a strict code of conduct once indoors.

It would appear that Mrs Jones had taken a liking to me. She made a fuss of me as she served up supper, then she allowed her daughter and I to spend some time together in the front parlour prior to saying goodnight to each other.

The next day, not only did I feel a strong attachment to Mai, something else had affected me and caught me off balance. It was the warmth and closeness of her tightly knit family in which motherly love was in abundance. It had caused a surge of envy to take hold of me.

The loud music of the military brass band and the shouting of "bon voyage" from family members on the Southampton quayside resembled a story-book setting. Viewing the crowds from my top-deck vantage point, I felt a buzz of excitement at my imminent departure, but also, in view of the emotional scenes below, I wondered how intense my own feelings would have been if I had had somebody to wave me goodbye like Jenny or Mai.

***

With the dockside memories now distant and the tumultuous swell of the Bay of Biscay having passed, at last I began to settle into a troopship existence. This new life, including my recent sightings of Mediterranean dolphins and a succession of unbelievable sunsets, was proving to be the adventure of a lifetime.

I have so many recollections from this time, including the different locations where the ship dropped its anchor – Port Said, the Suez Canal, Colombo and Singapore, and on the return journey a day on the seashore at Aden where with shark safety-nets out at sea, I had enjoyed a swim in the warm waters of the Indian Ocean.

One particular memory was when our outward-bound ship arrived at Singapore. During the early evening the whole sky lit up with flashes of zigzag lightning; an event, I remember thinking, that marked my induction to the tropical climes.

***

Almost seven months to the day and with a kitbag full of memories, so to speak, I arrived back in the UK in time for the planned regimental march-past in Manchester, a celebratory event marking the historic coronation of Queen Elizabeth the Second.

In the meantime, however, there were two weeks of home leave to be enjoyed, a period I was looking forward to if only to show my friends and colleagues my tanned skin and sun-bleached hair.

Having learned from one of my sister's letters of the Seymours' impending move to a new address - a semi-detached, three-bedroomed property in a Manchester suburb – it came as no surprise that I found myself in full agreement with my mother's choice – a house with a back garden and a garage and "more importantly", as she pointed out, "a French door that opens out to the garden".

My mother's pride in her new acquisition created an atmosphere in which a new sense of harmony and a new beginning seemed achievable, especially where she and her daughter were concerned. And my new 'box' bedroom was not only warm and cosy, it had a feeling of security and belonging that felt tailor-made for a happy and contented future. With the satisfaction of having arranged everything to my own taste, and with my favourite music from my new Bush radio filling my bedroom, I lay on my bed in order to acclimatise myself to my new surroundings, and I was rewarded with one of the deepest and most relaxing sleeps of my life.

"You must have needed that! Aren't the army beds comfortable?"

Having told my father that my deep sleep was probably the result of having slept in a ship's hammock for a month, I then joined the rest of the family while they viewed their latest acquisitions – a black and white television and a piano. Had the lounge been twice the size, my mother would have chosen a baby grand, of that I was sure.

"We'll be able to watch you on television at next week's coronation parade, Jimmy!"

Sylvia's smile reflected her quiet humour; it also acknowledged the fact that there was finally a hint of family togetherness. Just how long it would last was another matter! With that same good feeling extending beyond the evening's supper-time, I retired to my bedroom in a state of happiness and contentment to count my blessings. Then I purposely directed my thoughts towards my recent overseas travelling. It was something I would never, ever forget.

Once my jungle training had been completed in the North of Malaya and having served out my time at the Penang barracks, I began my army career proper on the mainland at Butterworth. Here, in an attempt to get to know some of the local residents, I enlisted with a social/drama group at the nearby St Mark's Church. Several weeks were to pass before I became drawn to a beautiful-looking Eurasian girl called Sakinah who, with her long black hair, slim build and Chinese-style way of dressing, proved to be not only irresistible, but meeting her resulted in my seeking permission from her parents for our very first date.

Looking back to that day on the ferry as the two of

us crossed over to Mitchell Pier in Penang, I remember thinking how the local custom did not support any form of physical contact or the showing of feelings between the opposite sexes, which – on account of my wanting to link arms – seemed totally unfair.

Fortunately our date had included an afternoon at the cinema to watch the film premier of *The Robe*, where, having achieved our aims in the form of tightly clasped hands, we then exchanged our long-awaited first kiss.

But with all camp leave on hold due to increased terrorist activities and having served a short spell of filling in as a temporary company bugler, it seemed inevitable that weeks rather than days would have to be endured before being reunited with Sakinah.

On a day that will forever stay in my memory, a hot and humid day during which I had incinerated the bugs and insects on the office chairs and bed frames, an order came for me to report to the second in command's office.

"You might like to know, Private Seymour, that you have been requested to spend the weekend with one of the local families. I see no reason why you shouldn't go – so long as you're on your best behaviour at all times. Just remember, you're an ambassador of both the regiment and your country. Permission granted!"

Coming face to face with what appeared to be a bungalow on stilts, I soon met my weekend hosts. Beaming, they stepped down from their veranda, each taking turns to give me a warm handshake. Sakinah's father was obviously of European descent, whereas her mother's origins were probably a mixture of Malay and Chinese, a combination that had yielded such a beautiful-looking daughter. Aware that I was expected to be on my best behaviour and in an attempt to follow the rules, I decided to put on a show of good manners in the hope of impressing not only my hosts but also Sakinah.

Having noticed the black Morris car in the driveway and the way in which the family were dressed, I couldn't help but think that a sightseeing tour might be in the offing, something that immediately raised my spirits.

As if on the same wavelength, Mr Bruyne finished off his glass of orange and declared, "We thought of taking you to Bukit Mertajam but we have since decided on Tanjong Bunga in Penang. I hope you've brought a pair of swimming shorts?"

In summing up my experience of that magical day –full of tropical beauty and clear, blue seas – I can only describe it as 'heaven on earth'. Those were my thoughts as I lay on my bed at night-time under a mosquito-net canopy. Lying on cooling crisp white sheets, I recaptured everything that had taken place. In particular I recalled the sandy beaches and swimming in a lagoon-like setting, an experience that was enhanced by Sakinah joining in with me. Regretfully, with both Father and Mother keeping a watchful eye, our underwater excursions became limited to the odd kiss, whereas if we had been on our own, I was certain both of us would have been a lot more daring. Refreshed and revitalised, and with the word "food" having been mentioned, we then set off from the Sandycroft resort towards Penang where, according to Sakinah's mother, the renowned open-air stalls sold food of every description.

Knowing of tomorrow's exciting itinerary - a session at the local tennis club and an inland visit to a native Malay settlement - I found it impossible to go to sleep; though the sandalwood fragrance wafting through the warm night air and Sakinah's presence at the opposite end of the hallway were also responsible for keeping me awake.

No sooner had the weekend expired and no sooner had I settled into my routine back at the camp HQ than an order was issued to the effect that all camp leave had been suspended for one month. On top of this, when the opportunity did arrive for a reunion with Sakinah, I became informed of a temporary ban being in place owing to an infectious illness in the family. Finally, having fulfilled my aim in the form of another weekend pass – an achievement that had caused my excitement to soar - a bombshell landed in the form of a regimental news-sheet; it seemed the battalion had been deployed back to the UK.

Having returned temporarily to the present via the interruption of my father's coughing fit, I made a quick attempt to pick up the threads that had led to my final farewell to Sakinah, a sad moment when I had promised to return to Malaya on completion of my national service.

If only I could have stayed long enough to attend the wedding that Sakinah and I had been invited to, I thought. *And if only I had had the opportunity to share in more intimate moments with her.*

Fate, it would appear, had not been in my favour, but at least I had the memories of our time together. I also had the photograph she gave me and that treasured wedding invitation to the local St Mark's Church.

***

"Sylvia's bringing a gentleman home for tea on Sunday so, whatever you do, look your best. I don't think those new shoes you've bought will be suitable for the occasion either!"

My mother's reference to my footwear - something I was very proud of – was her way of saying that she didn't approve of my new, green-suede 'beetle-crusher' shoes, the ones I had bought specially for the Ashton Palais jiving sessions.

"How about wearing your brogues and your tailor-made sports jacket? That would be much more suitable."

Following a day of household chores in readiness for the guest's arrival, plus a final inspection from - as Sylvia would have put it – 'Her Ladyship', the time came for a relaxing interlude by the fireside. I took the opportunity to listen to my sister's favourite music records.

"Not too loud, Jimmy, otherwise we won't be able to hear the doorbell."

No sooner had I obliged my mother than into the lounge walked my sister, who, with a beaming smile, began the process of introducing the tall visitor who accompanied her.

"This is Geoffrey!"

By the time it was my turn to shake hands, I had not only concluded that Geoffrey was the best-looking boyfriend by far, there was something about him that reminded me of a certain film star – one who had played leading roles in a variety of war films. No wonder my mother looked pleased with herself! What with his great height, his uniform and a personality befitting that of a royal equerry, he seemed perfect! That he was an officer in the Fleet Air Arm was obvious but as to his rank, I wasn't sure and I couldn't ask him. What did go through my mind was how on earth Sylvia had come across him, especially with him being so upper class... I surmised that they must have met at the Ritz ballroom; that's where most service personnel gathered, especially the American servicemen.

No sooner had he been informed of my own involvement in the armed forces - something he seized upon as a way of lightening the atmosphere - he politely began questioning me about my experiences which, although humble compared to his, turned out to be less of an ordeal to express than I had imagined.

With the conversation having been interrupted by refreshments, it wasn't long before my mother focussed on something that might just create the impression she so desired.

"What do you think of my tea service, Geoffrey? It was a gift from Jimmy – all the way from Singapore."

What my mother had failed to disclose, for whatever reason, was that the Chinese-style embroidered silk jacket that Sylvia was wearing was another of my presents.

Due to the day's warm weather and my mother's need for space to prepare a teatime meal, she suggested opening the French doors, a move that couldn't have been better timed considering the amount of cigarette smoke that now filled the lounge. Our removal to the lawn proved to be my salvation; not only was I beginning to feel like a spare part, it provided an opportunity to escape from what I saw as being an over-the-top performance by my parents. Their falseness always made me cringe.

But for Sylvia and her boyfriend, I could have been

enjoying myself on my bike. With that thought still uppermost in my mind and having survived the most boring Saturday afternoon ever, it was little wonder that I arrived at the table before anyone else.

If first impressions were anything to go by, the chances were that Geoffrey wouldn't fail to be astounded by the amount and quality of the food on the table, especially in view of the food-rationing restrictions. From a choice of freshly made sandwiches, including a side salad, a bowl of fresh fruit, a mouth-watering trifle with fresh cream and a selection of cakes, it really was a feast to behold.

As the meal progressed, so did the atmosphere. This was undoubtedly a tribute to my mother's artistic culinary skills and her successful orchestration of the day. Also, judging by the mealtime conversation, it seemed certain that Geoffrey had effortlessly won over my parents… not that there had been any doubts about that. In fact, I could almost picture word for word my mother's comments to her husband, once the happy-looking couple had departed.

"Sylvia's struck gold with that one! What lovely manners he's got, not to mention his background."

Feeling the effects of a full stomach was one of the reasons I volunteered to wash-up; the other was to escape the cigarette smoke and the after-dinner conversation, something I regarded as being beyond me.

Finally, and having excused myself from the afternoon's proceedings, I was able to mount my bicycle and set off for some much-needed space. This also allowed me time to concentrate on my sister's future. As far as I was aware, the word 'marriage' hadn't been mentioned and yet, taking a leaf from my mother's book, I was already imagining a wedding taking place and even making future visits to her and Geoffrey's new home in Buckinghamshire.

With my own future very much on the agenda – that is, a return to the regimental barracks in order to continue with my administrative duties – the prospect, compared to my recent overseas experiences, was unappealing to say the least. On the plus side, though, and with the ability to don civilian clothes instead of a uniform, there was every chance of using my evening leave in order to pursue a now favourite pastime of mine – the weekly rock 'n' roll dancing at the local palais.

***

By the time August had arrived not only had I learned of my sister's breakup with the handsome Fleet Air Arm officer – a huge disappointment to my parents - I had also received exciting news of the regiment's latest tour of duty, which caused my hopes to rise at the prospect of yet more overseas travel. We were set for Berlin.

"You must promise me that you'll be on your guard where girls are concerned. I don't want any more irritated fathers coming to the house, wanting to know of your intentions towards their daughters!"

Unbeknown to my parents was the recent episode whereby a girl I had met at the palais had taken me to her house for afternoon tea in order to meet her mother and father, a visit that in view of the strong crush she had on me, I now regretted.

Sooner rather than later, and having found myself included in the imminent advance party, I found myself attending what was a last-minute treat by my parents and my sister – a meal at the Queen's Hotel in

Manchester. Here, apart from being subjected to yet more advice, I picked up on an ongoing rift between Sylvia and her mother. Noting the intensity of their argumentative exchanges, I learned that not only was Sylvia's recent break-up still being debated; it was as if she would never, ever be forgiven for having rejected Geoffrey's approaches. It seemed that all of her mother's efforts had been for nothing.

Knowing what a private person my sister was, there was very little chance of my ever finding out the reason behind her decision – not that it really concerned me. All I knew was that behind the tinted spectacles my mother was wearing, there would be the tell-tale signs of her anguish, which no doubt would be inflicted on us both. My posting couldn't come soon enough.

Chapter Eight

The coincidence of early-morning sunshine just as I arrived in Berlin seemed like a good omen for the weeks and months that were to lie ahead. But little did I know just how much good fortune I was to encounter, as almost from the word 'go' and after having completed the first day's settling-in process at the barracks, I was invited to join a night-time excursion to a local hotspot - a cellar bar with a jukebox.

From the first moment of entering the premises I felt an excitement like no other. It was unlike my time in Penang when I had complied with every rule going concerning good behaviour and being a good ambassador for the regiment; now I felt totally free and unrestricted. Maybe it was the effect of the German ale, being a lot stronger than the Tiger beer I'd sampled in Malaya. However, the combination of blaring music and alcohol, plus the arrival of two good-looking young females who joined us, made me feel as if this moment had been waiting for me and all that was now required was my participation.

Her name was Erika – an attractive girl, to say the least, who introduced herself and chose the seat next to mine before signalling to the waiter for another round of drinks. Her composure and her outgoing friendliness towards the bar's occupants seemed to indicate a person of great popularity and as I warmed to her presence I couldn't help but notice the many acknowledgements that she and her friend responded to.

"This is my best friend Elsa!"

As I shook her hand I became aware of the huge

grin on my mate's face, being an indication that he also had 'clicked'.

"I think I will call you Jems. I like that name best."

Whether it was down to her accent or her mispronunciation, I wasn't sure, but she could have called me anything she liked, such was my growing infatuation with this beautiful stranger. Her spellbinding influence was beginning to cause all kinds of strange feelings inside me. Following another beer and a schnapps I found myself being guided to the small dance area in front of the jukebox, where, with Erika's choice of music having been selected, I drew as close to her as was possible in a clinch that signalled our desire for each other. As the lights dimmed in the now crowded room, she whispered something in my ear and although most of the sentence was inaudible, I did manage to grasp what she meant by her use of the word 'leibling', a phrase I assumed meant 'darling', and by the way in which she was guiding me towards the exit. Under the influence of alcohol and with a desire to fulfil my ultimate goal, I willingly allowed myself to be propelled towards some nearby bushes, where without a moment's thought or hesitation I succumbed to Erika's seduction.

The giveaway smile of contentment that accompanied my return to the cellar bar proved sufficient for Erika's friend to make a comment and, as I listened to their conversation interspersed with gestures and smiles, it became apparent that I had proved worthy of Erika's expectations. With a promise to meet again at the weekend, I returned to the barracks in a state of euphoria where, unable to sleep, I purposely brought to mind every delicious detail of everything that had transpired.

To think that I had thrown caution to the wind - including my mother's advice – and now, not only had I lost my virginity, the whole experience had opened up an exciting new chapter in my life, a chapter that was the complete opposite of my yesteryear.

Erika had many admirers but it was me who, in her opinion, was best suited for what she had in mind for the future – something I realised when I unexpectedly received a parcel that had been left for me at the guardroom. Presuming the sender to be Erika - especially with the brightly coloured ribbon tied around it - I eventually opened the wrapping to expose a cake and a note with the words 'Liebchen - Happy Birthday'. My reaction, instead of displaying excitement at Erika's thoughtfulness, was to focus on what I viewed to be the strangest of coincidences; as I brought Mai's image and my previous birthday to mind, my thoughts were transported all the way back to Porthmadog.

"I hope you're going to share that with us?"

The repeated requests of my army pals for a slice of cake brought me back to earth and reminded me of the comments some of them had made about getting too involved – of course many of the girls were looking for a husband and a new way of life.

Declaring myself to be much too young for a permanent relationship, I told Erika that I wanted to finish with her, a decision she surprisingly accepted. Explaining that she understood the reason and with a promise that she would wait until I changed my mind, she made me agree to accompany her one last time. She added, "Especially because of the plans I have for you – a visit to the countryside."

It was whilst I was waiting at the tram stop on the Heerstrasse on that Sunday that I compared the fresh-air setting of the day with the smoke-filled atmosphere of Erika's night world. It was a contrast so black and white that I began to wonder how she would cope with the overhead sunshine.

If nothing else, I couldn't thank her enough for having found the perfect place in which to enjoy the picnic she had arranged. It was a shaded beauty spot in the beautiful Gatow Forest where, having spent an afternoon strolling hand-in-hand beneath the trees, we both gave in to our shared desire for each other.

Lying in bed that same evening with sleep a million miles away, I couldn't help but feel closer to Erika than at any other time, something that shouldn't have been the case considering that today was supposedly our last time together. In spite of this and the ageing lines she had exposed as a result of wearing less make-up, I still couldn't bring myself to call time on a relationship that had proved so irresistible.

By Christmas time of that same year and in the knowledge that my tour of duty was nearing completion, I began the task of saying goodbye to all of my friends and colleagues, including the one and only Erika, who, still convinced that she and I had a future together, even to the point of us being reunited in England, refused point-blank to accept my departure.

The eventual outcome – Erika's emotional outburst - was something that stuck in my mind ever since leaving Berlin. Aided by the train's rhythmic clattering as it journeyed through eastern Germany towards Holland, and under the watchful gaze of the Russian guards, I once again relived that moment at the barrack gates when it had been time for the bus to depart. No sooner had the vehicle set off than, with a shudder as the brakes were applied, it had come to a sudden halt again. As I looked through the front window it became clear that a pedestrian had caused a near catastrophe by standing in the road – something I thought of as being silly and irrational. With the regimental guards having escorted the person onto the pavement and the all-clear having been given, the bus slowly pulled away from the kerb. As I looked through the side window to view the culprit, I came face-to-face with a pleading and tearful Erika, who having finally caught my attention flashed a look of stone-faced contempt at me.

With a feeling of guilt haunting my every thought, and with the Russian soldier glancing in my direction, I turned my attention to the train's blacked-out windows, an outlook that in every way matched my sombre mood.

There was a definite resemblance between the Russian guard and someone I knew – someone who had a similar blank stare and who was devoid of emotion... As a way of extinguishing that pained look on Erika's face from my mind, I searched my memory for clues as to the identity of the person I was looking for, a task that slowly but surely produced a breakthrough. Pinpointing the person in question I then retraced my thoughts back to the notorious Spandau Prison in West Berlin, where, in compliance with my regimental requirements, I had served a whole week of guard duty.

It's strange how a troop of soldiers was required to stand guard over two people, I thought.

Of course, it was common knowledge that they were war criminals but even so, to me it had seemed so unnecessary. As daunting as it had been, I never did find out who was who, out of the pair of them.

However, one thing was sure, the memory of that fleeting moment when I had observed the person in question – the man whose expression had left its mark on me - was what I had recalled.

Whilst my fellow comrades struggled for a good night's sleep, soothed a little by the rhythmic swaying of the carriage, I began reconnecting with my Berlin experiences, instigated by the insignia on the Russian guard's tunic. Absorbed by the similarity between him and his fellow guards at the Brandenburg Gate, I recalled the day when I had been privileged to be included in a bus tour to the Eastern sector of the city, a journey whose climax was the breathtaking vista of the famed Russian 'Garden of Remembrance'. As opposed to the blackened ruins that I had witnessed on the way to the monument – a stark reminder of the Battle of Berlin – the Russian cemetery stood out like a beacon of modern-day architecture. It was an amazing design, to say the least. But even more astounding was the man-made hill with its white steps leading to the top, which once climbed revealed the centrepiece of the whole design - a giant statue of a Russian soldier and a small child. Something else I experienced on that day was the still atmosphere throughout the gardens, one heavy with the weight of what might have taken place there.

Meanwhile with Christmastime approaching and an end to my military career in sight, the thought of resuming life as a civilian couldn't come soon enough – not that I had any regrets. My national service had been without doubt the best thing that had ever happened to me. The experiences and memories I had accumulated had given me treasures in abundance.

***

"His name is Aleksy Crushelski and he's a doctor from Poland." As my sister laughingly corrected my pronunciation of the strange-sounding name, she added, "I don't think Her Ladyship approves of him, at all!"

Within the space of four weeks I had not only re-established my work routine in the city, I also had been reunited with friends and acquaintances and the ever-complicated social life of my sister Sylvia. On the face of it and having met the so-called Doctor Crushelski in person, I could not help but warm to the sincerity and genuineness that he so effortlessly displayed, and - surprisingly, owing to his status and profession – my sister's love for him. I even considered the possibility of his becoming a future brother-in-law.

Why my mother saw him as being unsuitable for her daughter didn't make sense, especially as he was a doctor. The more my sister continued with her pursuit, the more my mother made her objections felt until, following an upsetting, tearful climax, the balding yet handsome doctor disappeared off the scene for good.

Confiding in me one day, as she sometimes did when looking for support, my mother tried in earnest to convince me that it had been for the best, adding, "You know, he (the doctor) was at that camp in Wales – the one where all the foreigners were kept during and after the war? Plus he was a staunch Catholic!"

As usual, due to my general ignorance and my desire to keep the peace, I eventually accepted my mother's explanation as being in my sister's best interests, although in line with my father's opinion, there was a suspicion that my mother's view had been more of a personal issue. I often thought to myself that if it hadn't been for the advent of television, my sister's private life would have been subjected to more inquisitions than it already was, whereas, owing to the welcoming distraction of the small screen, the atmosphere in the home improved enormously.

With my own life back to its old routine and with a good helping of additional sports and musical interests, my capacity for living life to the full increased. Having now passed my driving test, I also had good cause to celebrate my very latest achievement. But in a matter of days my jubilations had all but expired when, following a late-night bus journey home, my world came to a shuddering full stop.

"Jimmy! Jimmy, wake up!"

Those pleading words from my sister as I slowly recovered consciousness not only aided my initial recovery, they became imprinted on my mind to such an extent that even two days later I could still hear her desperate call. Now, confined to bed in order to recuperate – a restriction supervised by my mother – I found myself continuously attempting to piece together the events of the night in question. That I had been in a collision with a tree was clear, but I spent many moments wondering how it had come about. What I did remember was stepping off a late-night trolley bus in a state of over-excitement, having just passed my audition for the famed Hallé Choir. With all kinds of possibilities buzzing around my head, I absentmindedly began running along the avenue towards my home. That was it! In the darkness of the night, a sudden collision had ensued, followed by a complete blackout.

How long I had lain unconscious remained unclear

but, assuming that the next late-night bus to arrive was five or ten minutes later, that must have been the length of time I had been out cold. How lucky for me that my very own sister had returned home at that precise moment – an unbelievable coincidence in itself.

Only later was I to find out that Sylvia had managed to catch the next bus after mine, and as a result it had been her who had found me lying in a heap and unconscious. Hers was the face that had come into view as she kneeled down on the pavement beside me. I was in no position to respond but I could faintly hear her frantic shouts of, "Jimmy, Jimmy! Wakeup, Jimmy!"

Aided by a neighbour who had responded to my sister's cries, somehow I was carried to the nearby doctor's house where, following a series of urgent bangs on his door, the pyjama-clad doctor admitted us into his surgery.

"You look as though you've been kicked by a mule," were his first words.

Looking back on the drama of that night and the coincidence of my sister's timely arrival on the scene, it would appear that, discounting my severe bruising and two black eyes, I could count myself as being very lucky.

Now that the nausea and headaches had subsided and because of my continuing improvement, I was finally able to think more clearly. In fact, with my other sister in mind, I began focussing on the comedy of my accident. How many times had I heard Vera mention the scar on my forehead, the result of having fallen out of my pram as a baby? Then there was the other scar on my head, the one incurred when throwing a large stone up into a conker tree! Luckily, my injury this time was to be scar-free.

For some reason, I recalled yet another incident, one that had been kept locked away with all the other secrets of my past. Even now I can still feel the painful impact of my forehead colliding with cold brickwork. It was a moment of madness on my part, especially knowing now what the consequences could have been. I think it was around the time of my twelfth birthday and a few months after my father had died. Looking back on the occasion, I would say that the purposeful banging of my head against the wall in order to create a bruise for someone to notice was a desperate cry for attention and an inner plea for some tiny morsel of affection.

"You stupid boy!"

The house mother's reaction on seeing my bruised forehead turned out to be just the opposite of what I had hoped for and instead of a caress and the appliance of butter to make it better, I received a reprimand for not looking where I was going. With hindsight, I should have known that in the loveless world of the institution the chances of a cuddle and a show of affection were miniscule.

***

"Jimmy! Are you awake, Jimmy?"

With my reminiscing now over and the soft tapping on my bedroom door growing louder, I invited Sylvia into my room to ask what the urgency was about; after all, I had already said goodnight to her.

"I forgot to tell you, I bought you a record today," she said as she sat on the bed. "You can play it on the radiogram tomorrow. I know you'll like it. It reminded me of you when you were little. It's called 'The Jimmy Brown Song'."

Over the next few days that recording by a French singing group became firmly imprinted on my mind. I loved the simplicity of the words and its haunting melody. My other favourite pop songs were temporarily eclipsed by the verse 'All the chapel bells were ringing'.

By the Saturday of that week and feeling more like my old self, I began preparing for my long-awaited bicycle ride into the countryside. If I was lucky, I might even stumble across an undiscovered and exciting archaeological barrow.

"Before you go, Jimmy, I want you to do something for me."

Unsure of what was coming next – an unexpected sense of harmony had prevailed for some days – I looked into my mother's troubled face expecting a request for help and support in connection with Sylvia. It wouldn't be the first time she'd sought my involvement in order to achieve her aims, especially when trying to overrule my sister's decisions.

"Sit down whilst I try to explain. It's about your father. He won't tell you himself, but whenever he hears that 'Jimmy Brown' song that you play, it upsets him. He feels personally let down by the fact that having given you a new start in life, including the family name... well, what I'm trying to say is, it's like throwing everything back in his face."

That my father's feelings had been hurt came as a shock. To rectify the situation immediately, I told her that I wouldn't play the song any more – even though I knew her story wasn't true.

In my heart I knew that saying goodbye to the song would be an impossibility – especially now that

I had formed an attachment to its words and music. In any case, it was as much my sister's record as mine, which meant I would have to find a good hiding place for it.

With yet another piece of mind-clutter to offload, I finally set off for the freedom of the outdoors with the 'Jimmy Brown' music accompanying me in my head.

At the dinner table that same evening I was given a surprise present by my mother. Handing me a brown-paper parcel, she informed me that it was a framed picture for my bedroom. My reaction to the contents – including the antique frame – was that it was a bribe for having obliged her earlier request.

"Why don't you hang it next to the other one I bought you?" she asked. "They'd go well together, don't you think?"

Before dimming my bedroom light that evening, I spent a few moments alternating my gaze between the two pictures – 'The Light of the World' painting and poem on one wall and Kipling's 'If' on the other. The trouble was, they had the effect of making me feel that my mother was in the same room – a thought that made me feel most uncomfortable.

Or, I suddenly thought, *could it be the guilt I'm feeling in connection with my latest flirtation?* It was an affair that my mother would be appalled at!

The female in question was one of the older nurses at my mother's place of work. She had accepted my mother's advice regarding my giving her driving lessons.

If only my mother knew the half of it! I thought.

What had begun as an innocent relationship between driver and pupil had turned into irresistible, passion-filled intervals of desire that caused me to think of nothing else most of the time.

Chapter Nine

The more I thought about my life, the more I was reminded that just like my sister I was treading that same pathway of secretiveness and deception, which although alien to my simple way of going about things proved to be the only answer to my mother's constant inquisition-like questioning.

During a year in which my football and cricket skills were perfected to first-team status, and due to my company's first-division standing in both leagues, I not only enjoyed the benefits of extra time off work, I was able to widen my geographic knowledge by travelling to different venues in the county.

In the meantime and because of the extra part-time modelling work my sister was taking on, her beauty appeared to intensify with every photographic encounter. Her looks and mannequin-type outfits were, to my mind, testimony to the 'beauty queen' description that my friends and colleagues referred to. That said, Sylvia's private life – an unknown mystery as ever - was becoming a cause for major concern for her parents. Having been thwarted in her attempts to control her daughter's choice of men friends, my mother now threatened a reprisal by way of locking her out of the home.

"Your sister's gone!"

This disclosure by my tearful mother some two weeks later came as a surprise. I somehow felt cheated by Sylvia's disappearance and by the fact that she had not confided in me.

Then again, I thought to myself, *with Sylvia's personal life being beyond my comprehension, plus the fact that we both lead very different lifestyles, why would she tell me?*

The result was that I now had to contend with a mother who professed to be broken-hearted and sick with worry. As the days passed by, the house felt as if it were deep in mourning. Unable to accept the loss of her daughter, my mother resorted to going through my sister's personal belongings in her bedroom and in any other hiding places of hers to discover her whereabouts. She phoned various friends and acquaintances and as a last resort, my sister's place of work.

As the days progressed and having assumed that my mother had come to terms with her loss, I was shocked to learn that my mother's 'look-out' accomplices had located my sister's whereabouts. They also revealed the person with whom she was living. As expected from a person who refused to let go, my mother embarked on a two-week strategy of writing pleas by letter, until…

"Jimmy, would you please do something for me? You don't have to, if you don't want to."

It would appear that as a result of the swelling beneath both her eyes, not to mention her worried looks, my mother was nearing the end of her tether. With my father at work and no one else to turn to, and aware of the fact that her display of tears was having the desired effect, I agreed to help her. But as today was a sunny Saturday, I had planned on a bike ride to see a female acquaintance, a date I had been really looking forward to.

"I know it will interfere with your arrangements, Jimmy, but we've got to try and get Sylvia out of the mess she's in. She's living in a bedsit with a man who's a boxer – a horrible man who's dragging her down into the gutter. I've got the address here,

Jimmy. It's near to the High Street baths in Manchester."

Armed with the details of Sylvia's address and with an uneasy feeling about having agreed to help, I boarded the city-bound bus in a state of apprehension. Already I could feel myself having second thoughts – especially knowing that Sylvia's partner was a boxer!

I arrived in the High Street area some thirty minutes later and having pinpointed the location in question, I tentatively climbed the steps of a tenement-style building, one that was divided into individual flats. With a final glance at my mother's written instructions and a tense short interval of "Should I or shouldn't I?" I eventually willed myself to give the most timid of knocks on the door.

After a few seconds of silence, during which time I congratulated myself on nobody being at home, the door was suddenly opened by my sister who was completely thrown off her guard by my presence. Coyly she invited me into the room.

Seemingly lost for words at my surprise visit, she stood awkwardly staring at her drab surroundings, thus creating a moment's pause for me to deliver my message.

"Your mother's asked me to tell you she's sorry and she wants you to come home."

With a feeling of relief that I had accomplished my mission, I waited for Sylvia's reaction, one that I hoped would be short and sweet, thus allowing me to make my way home in time for my bike ride.

"Just go, sonny boy, before I do something I might regret!"

From behind a curtained area in the corner of the room, a thick-set man appeared. Judging by the look on his face, there was every chance I could become a victim of his anger. Fortunately my sister manoeuvred herself into a position between her man friend and the exit, prompting me to make a quick retreat. But those brief moments allowed just enough time for me to absorb her look of helplessness.

Burdened with the thought that he could have swatted me like a fly on the wall, I thankfully made my way to the bus stop, thinking about how it might have ended if Sylvia hadn't intervened – something I quickly dismissed from my mind.

My mother's reaction on learning of her daughter's living arrangements was one of utter despair.

"It won't last, you'll see! I'll give it another two weeks and then she'll be begging to come home."

I tried not to think about what my sister's future might hold. I felt I had already interfered in her personal affairs. *If only I could turn the clock back*, I thought.

With my mind awash with all that had transpired, I gladly seized the opportunity to escape to the countryside and as I pedalled my way onto the main highway and into a cooling afternoon breeze, I immediately felt the relief of having left all of my problems behind me.

However, in one small corner of my mind was the nagging thought that my meddling might have damaged the relationship between me and my sister. As I contemplated the long-term effects it might have, I quietly prayed that she would understand my 'piggy-in-the-middle' position and not hold anything against me.

Almost a month after that episode and to the delight of my parents – my mother especially – Sylvia made her long-expected return to the family home. To my great relief, there was an unusual absence of any comment whatsoever from our mother.

***

With a return to more normal conditions in the home, I decided it was time for a reunion with my other sister Vera, someone I hadn't spoken with for a long time.

"You won't believe it, Jimmy, but I've found out where our mother is."

My first reaction was to think, *What a coincidence!* Here I was, having made the decision to walk across the city during my lunch break, to be confronted by my over-excited sister, anxious to divulge everything she had learned about our mother's circumstances.

"I've been given permission to have her visit this coming Saturday afternoon. Sylvia's coming and I hope you'll come too."

This was going to be a very unusual day in my life – a family reunion. I was filled with intrigue, but I also remembered that Sylvia and I had agreed not to say anything to Mr and Mrs Seymour for fear of causing any upset.

This, my first visit to Vera and her husband's house, presented an ideal opportunity to congratulate them both on their marriage – a celebration that had taken place without me, owing to my national service commitments.

How strange it all seemed. Here I was, sat in an armchair, wondering what my mother would look like, and both my sisters were on the settee chatting about fond memories of their childhood years.

The long-awaited knock on the front door caused an outburst of emotions between my sisters. Then I witnessed their anxious looks as they hugged our mother before leading her into the sitting room. It was a very touching scene.

My own introduction to the small, elderly, grey-haired lady was awkward; I was lost for words. My "Hello, Mother" and a handshake seemed totally inadequate for such a momentous occasion.

Addressed as 'Sylvia' – the same name as her daughter – she (my mother), following a cup of tea and some cakes, launched herself into a non-stop conversation regarding the buses she had travelled on from the workhouse, an achievement she proudly boasted of. With that off her chest, so to speak, she then withdrew to her inner self, with there being seemingly no need for any more chatter. Instead, she resorted to smoking her Woodbine cigarettes which, with unsteady hands, she offered to her fellow smokers - my sister Sylvia and Vera's husband.

Judging by my mother's looks, she had obviously been attractive in her younger days – much like her daughters – but as I tried to make a connection with her, I realised I had nothing in common with her except a few family features.

Latching on to the way my sisters spoke to her, during a conversation about her seamstress duties at the workhouse hospital, I began to realise the intensity of her institutionalisation, something I was more than familiar with. It wasn't just the child-like responses my mother gave that concerned me, it was the way in which she seemed totally distant when smiling - something that made me think she was unable to comprehend what was taking place.

By the time of Sylvia's and my departure, I had not only been made aware of my mother's plight, I had also learned that owing to her depression, plus the long-term effects of her medication, she would more than likely have to remain in the workhouse, a fact that caused me to feel both guilt and sadness at the same time.

***

"It's time to go, Jimmy!"

Taking great care as I eased myself onto the rear seat of the car, I made myself comfortable for the long journey ahead, one that would terminate at my mother's favourite holiday resort – not that I hadn't visited Blackpool before now. This last-minute holiday to enjoy the year's illuminations had been planned due to my immobility, caused by an accident whilst playing football.

Thank goodness, I thought, *that it happened now and not in six weeks' time for my 21st birthday!*

What surprised me, as I considered my broken ankle, was why it had been necessary to cover my whole leg in a plaster cast. For the umpteenth time, I cursed the football match in which I had sustained the injury. My social life had also suffered as a result, and now – in view of my limited movements – my usual fun-filled activities had all but disappeared.

But who would have thought that later, despite the incapacitation and pain, I would end up celebrating what had been an astonishing holiday? Not that my parents had known anything about it. If it hadn't been for their insistence on my having a downstairs room at the hotel, my good fortune may never have come about…

My lucky encounter had taken place indoors rather than outdoors and it had all begun when the landlady had brought me a tray of food to my room. Because of my disability I had been given the lower of the two bunks, meaning that, in order to serve me, she had had to bend down to avoid the upper bed frame. Unfortunately as she straightened up, she hit her head and this resulted in her feeling dazed. Suddenly she fell, not only on top of me but also on top of my midday meal. Trying to help, I reached out to where she was holding her head and as I did so, she squeezed my arm as an acknowledgement of my concern.

"No doubt I'll have a bump on my head after this. I'm sorry about your lunch. I'll bring you another one later, once I've recovered and cleared up this mess."

As she got to her feet, she leaned over and kissed my forehead, remarking, "I'm sorry if I hurt your leg when I fell on you. I'll try and make it up to you with the next offering."

Within seconds of her departure, I mourned the loss of my meal as I was so hungry. I also sensed something about the landlady that I couldn't quite explain, something that, the more I thought about it, revealed a generous and warm-hearted person who appeared to be motherly in every sense of the word.

"Here we are, Jimmy, some freshly made sandwiches and a nice piece of cake. I'll put the tray on the cabinet whilst we make you comfortable. I'll try not to bang my head this time!"

As she leaned over me in order to straighten my backrest, I immediately became aware of her femininity; not only had her blouse conveniently opened, she took hold of my hand and placed it across her large bosom. Smiling into my eyes, she invitingly urged me to participate.

Having handled the 'forbidden fruits' with both hands and experienced the full-on warm kisses that had been offered, I lay awake that same night thinking of nothing else but that exciting interlude, the one that had produced the sensation of my having been seduced by an experienced and mature woman.

By the time of the Saturday-morning goodbyes, one that included my mother thanking the landlady for looking after me, we finally set off on our long journey, an excursion I could hardly wait for considering the store of memories I wanted to savour.

Strangely enough, whilst passing the South Shore funfair - a place that under normal circumstances I would most certainly have visited – I began to realise how much this particular holiday had benefitted me and how a certain distraction had helped in overcoming my injury.

With the blare from a Johnny Ray record filling the house and a seemingly relaxed and carefree Sylvia awaiting our arrival, it appeared that she too had benefitted from her own week's holiday – a week in Oostende with her friend Rose.

The coincidence of my sister's holiday being at the same time as ours smelled strongly of my mother's interference, especially knowing of her distrust of Sylvia. However, with a good-natured harmony uniting us, we all sat round the teatime table in order to share our holiday experiences and, of course, the details of my injured leg.

A few weeks hence and with my rehabilitation complete, I decided that instead of making a return to football I would instead concentrate on my music and piano, it being a more sensible option. Besides, as well as my involvement in the annual 'Messiah' concert with the Hallé Orchestra and Choir, a local operatic society had also sought my participation in their winter-time production.

As ever, my social life involved lots of friendships with various females. One girl in particular from my place of work had become so smitten with me that she unexpectedly turned up on my doorstep, an event that – knowing of my mother's strict etiquette – caused me to panic.

"Come in," said my mother invitingly. "It's very rare I get to meet my son's girlfriends; he normally keeps them a secret."

From that moment on, not only did Her Ladyship quiz Barbara about her family background and where she lived, she also managed to extract the dimensions of her feelings towards me, which seemed to point in one direction only. The trouble was, I too felt the same way about Barbara and for the first time ever, I had actually begun to think about a future with her, especially as I had already met her down-to-earth and loving family.

"Thank you, Barbara, for coming to see us. It's been such a pleasure. I hope you'll call again sometime?"

Surprised by my mother's pleasantries, I then accompanied Barbara to her bus stop in the city, a journey that was filled with all kinds of wonderful feelings of togetherness, especially now that the ice had been broken with my mother.

But how could I have been so gullible as to think that my mother approved of my liaison with Barbara? Reprimanding myself for having been so stupid, I brought to mind the letter I had just received from Barbara's parents – a notification that informed me that I was no longer welcome at their house. It also stated that I was to stay away from their daughter.

"She wasn't for you anyway!" remarked my mother on learning of my disappointment. "You know she's from a council estate, don't you?"

Despite my 'deaf-ear' approach to my mother's comments, I still couldn't for the life of me make sense of any of it; I had only spent a lunchbreak with Barbara two days ago and everything had been fine then. But when we did finally bump into each other again, she accused me of two-timing her with another girl called Jeanette.

"And what about that other girl in the Hallé Choir, the one you went to the cinema with? According to your mother, you've got girlfriends all over the place!"

In spite of my protestations, our relationship was brought to a final conclusion by her hurtful accusations.

"I don't want to see you again, ever!" she said.

That my mother had interfered was obvious, especially after having heard Barbara's revelations about my supposed social activities.

For a whole week following that incident, I sulked over my loss and built up a resentment towards my mother that unfortunately spilled into anger. With a defiance that proclaimed my determination to try and rectify matters, I informed her that I was going to Barbara's house that very afternoon in order to make it up to her.

In what turned out to be a wasted journey across Manchester, and having had the family's front door slammed shut on me, not only did I feel hurt, I again blamed my interfering mother, a person who persistently used her cunning as a way of controlling both me and my sister.

"I'm so sorry, Jimmy, I accidently caught it whilst I was doing the dusting."

Having arrived home to a welcoming cup of tea

and a slice of cake – a peace offering, in my opinion – I noticed what looked like a pile of broken pottery on the sideboard. On closer inspection, it bore a marked resemblance to the much-admired china tea set I had sent from Singapore.

"I felt really upset when it happened and unfortunately it can't be mended. I hope you'll forgive me?"

With a begrudging "It's alright" I retreated to the garage as a way of escape, where, overcome with a ferocious anger, I set about cleaning every inch of my beloved bicycle.

Encouraged by the following morning's sunshine, I saddled up for what, if nothing else, would be a welcome ride into a countryside retreat, one that would not only help to clear my thoughts but, with luck, would help me to come to terms with the loss of Barbara.

With those thoughts foremost in my mind, I headed off to the surrounding hills, but instead of accepting the events of the last twenty-four hours, I inadvertently turned my thoughts towards the broken tea set and the apologies that had gone with it.

I wondered, *Could it really have been an accident, or was it more likely that she deliberately smashed it as revenge for going against her wishes?*

Chapter Ten

Interrupted by a tugging on my jacket sleeve, I returned to the present. My sister was pointing excitedly through the car window.

"We're nearly there, Jimmy! You'll be able to see the pleasure beach soon."

Sylvia realised that my interest lay solely in Blackpool's funfair and sampling the fairground rides rather than watching her in a beauty parade line-up. But the parade was still something I was looking forward to.

Perhaps, I thought to myself, *I could make use of my free pass into the open-air lido for the first part of the beauty parade and later sneak off unnoticed?*

As well as being Sylvia's big day, today was also the crowning glory of her parents – her mother especially, who, having encouraged her daughter to participate in the contest in the first place, was now but a few hours away from achieving her goal. Considering all the upsets, the strained atmosphere at home and the numerous late-night set-tos between mother and daughter, I just hoped it had all been worthwhile. My thoughts were aimed more at my mother, who, because of her constant disapproval of Sylvia's lifestyle, had caused herself to become ill with worry on more than one occasion. Not for the first time, I asked myself why it was that my sister chose to put up with all the upset rather than finding somewhere else to live; but then, knowing the extent of her mother's influence - and the way in which she bought Sylvia's affections by way of expensive clothing and jewellery – it wasn't really surprising that she remained.

The disappearance of my sister together with her manager was the cue for me and my parents to make our way to the VIP area which, because of its unique positioning behind the judges' table, provided us with what was bound to be a panoramic view. Weather-wise it couldn't have been a better day; not only had the clouds dispersed, the reflection of the sun's rays on the open-air pool together with the warm sea breeze provided an atmosphere that was in keeping with what was about to take place.

As each swim-suited contestant walked round the pool carrying their heart-shaped identity number – my sister included – it dawned on me how young some of the girls looked and, because of their high heels, how tall some of them were. As beautiful as my sister was, I couldn't help but consider the competition she was up against, noting in particular the taller, younger and more vivacious members of the line-up. The thought of the nearby roller coaster at the pleasure beach finally convinced me that it was time to make my escape and, having offered my apologies and with a promise to rendezvous after the competition, I joyously embarked on my afternoon's adventure.

Not until the evening meeting with my parents at the Tower Ballroom did I learn of my sister's results. My mother, in a protective and disgruntled manner, said, "Sylvia may not have been the best bathing beauty, but she was certainly the best in the fashion parade. Why the judges overlooked her, I'll never know."

Whilst feeling disappointed for my sister, my own afternoon had been one of pure joy and excitement. As opposed to sharing the gloom of the return journey home, I instead filled my mind with all the memories of the afternoon funfair and of course the unique experience of having been driven to the seaside and back in a Rolls Royce.

On what was going to be another new adventure – a summer-time climbing and camping holiday in Scotland – not only did I incur the displeasure of my mother for not having joined them on their particular vacation, I was also accused of being selfish to the point of thinking only of myself, something I couldn't for the life of me understand. True, for the past two years, apart from the odd week away with my parents, my main two-week holiday had been taken up with my Territorial Army commitments which, looking back on them, confirmed my belief that my army call-up had been the best thing ever to happen to me, especially as it had introduced me to the beautiful countryside of Wiltshire and Pembrokeshire.

Being the slow thinker that I was and unable to grasp the meaning behind some of my parents' remarks, I sometimes failed to comprehend the implications of a conversation, especially when my sister's personal life was under discussion.

"Of course!" I gasped.

Having reprimanded myself for not having thought of it earlier, I cast my mind back to a recent interchange between Sylvia and our mother when, with a raised voice, Her Ladyship had questioned my sister's ability to look after young children. It appeared that, together with her friend Rose, Sylvia had been offered a month's holiday abroad in the South of France where, apart from enjoying the sights, they would both be employed as nannies. With that being the only explanation I could think of, I began visualising how empty the house would feel in my sister's absence and the burden that would be put on me as a result of my mother's brooding. In addition, I inevitably sympathised with my adopted father, who, in his efforts to placate his wilful wife, always seemed to fall short in her eyes. Feeling sorry for my father had become a habit throughout the time I had been a member of this family and frequently, following an argument involving my sister, I had left the house thinking, *Rather you than me*.

***

In no time at all, it seemed, and with Christmas just around the corner, my thoughts turned towards tobogganing and the lure of the snow-capped hills. Also, I excitedly counted out the many rounds of parties I would be attending and, more to the point, the choice of girls who would be there.

"Sylvia's new man friend is coming this weekend so if you've made any arrangements, you'll have to cancel them."

My mother's insistence boiled down to the fact that she wanted to make a good impression with a united family gathering, especially as the guest was a Frenchman and, from her point of view, a person regarded as being a serious prospect. Usually Mother and Sylvia ended up in heated arguments or in a situation where for days neither one of them would speak to each other. On this occasion, however, it would appear that Her Ladyship was in full approval of the person my sister had met on holiday, especially as he was a well-travelled, film-set photographer.

"I am very pleased to meet you, Jimmy. Your sister is a very beautiful girl. I am very – how you say – 'appy to meet her."

Pierre's pronunciation of the letter 'j'(something that sounded like 'sj', as in 'je t'aime') made me smile. I also noted his friendly and sincere demeanour. Tall, slim and impeccably dressed, he certainly met with my parents' approval, and his foreign charm ensured a reception that had not been equalled since the episode of the now forgotten Fleet Air Arm officer.

Having kissed both the cheeks of His Lordship, Pierre proceeded to pay his respects to Her Ladyship by firstly kissing her proffered hand, followed by a flattering remark in which he made comparisons between hers and her daughter's looks.

Pierre's presence seemed to have brought the room to life and even though the lounge had been warmed by an open fire, there was a noticeable rise in the temperature, no doubt created by his charm.

"This is for you, Madame, and for Monsieur…"

The box of cigars that was handed to my father seemed huge, especially compared to the miniature-looking package that was offered to his wife.

Wasting no time in undoing the wrapping to see what was inside, my mother gasped in awe at what turned out to be her most favourite of French perfumes. Sensing that my sister had had a hand in the choice of gifts, I surveyed what was the most unusual of sights – a cheerful family gathering and a contentedness that even included Her Ladyship.

Had it not been for some kind of interim dispute between Sylvia and her mother, the whole weekend would have gone down as being the best I could remember. And as for Pierre, discounting his attempts to introduce me to the French game of 'Boulez', two things stood out as being his hallmark: his like for strong-smelling Camel cigarettes and the shaded spectacles he always wore. I was left with the impression that here was someone who was not only easy to get on with, he would also make a most suitable future brother-in-law.

Despite the buzz of excitement about my sister's potential future and the hope that from now on there would be an improved atmosphere in the home, Sylvia protested strongly at her mother's attempts to organise her life. She also made it known that she intended to spend her summer holiday abroad, a remark that further infuriated Her Ladyship. In an attempt to escape the unbearable atmosphere, I once again set off for the welcoming, stress-free outdoors – anything to get away from the unpleasantness between my sister and her mother.

At times like this I envied the man of the house – His Lordship – who, because of his demanding managerial role at work, conveniently absented himself from any involvement. Mind you, once he had eaten his evening meal, he would be informed in no uncertain terms of what had transpired that day and, as per usual, his wife's tears would be the result of her "selfish and ungrateful" daughter.

Since Sylvia and I rarely shared our feelings – a fact probably due to our age difference and being busy with our own lives, plus my mother's attempts to try to turn me against my sister – very few opportunities arose for us to forge a real brother-and-sister relationship… that was until one day during the springtime.

With nothing planned for the evening, or so it seemed, my sister unexpectedly asked me if I would go to the pictures with her.

"I'll pay," she said. "It's a film I've wanted to see for a long time. It's not a cowboy film but I'm sure you'll like it."

What Sylvia didn't tell me was that she had

already asked her friend Rose to come along. By the time the film had ended, I not only wished it hadn't been so boring, I also regretted the fact that it hadn't been shown in technicolour, as per the modern-day films. However, one thing that did inspire me was the film's music, being a haunting melody that I just couldn't get out of my mind. Whilst my sister's concentration had been very much focussed on the film's storyline, my own thoughts had instead become filled with the film's accompanying music.

Our cinema trip was to prove beneficial in more ways than one, in that not only did Sylvia introduce me to the music of Rachmaninoff, she also bought me the record of what she described as being the *Brief Encounter* music, which, whenever possible, we listened to with the volume turned up loud.

One other memory of that evening was my sister's reaction to the film's ending. This was a rare moment when I actually witnessed her dabbing her eyes with her handkerchief, which, bearing in mind her thick-skinned exterior, seemed unusual to say the least.

Once again, following what had been a relatively peaceful atmosphere at home, I became the go-between for my sister and her mother, whose relationship had for some reason reached breaking point.

"I want you to go into town and give this to Sylvia. If you get a chance to speak to her, please tell her that I'm very sorry and that I'll make it up to her when she comes home."

My mother's tear-stained face and puffed-up eyes were a reminder of the midnight arguing that had continued into the early hours and had kept me awake for ages. The peace offering – a sandwich and a piece of cake, all nicely wrapped – was, I was assured, a gift that Sylvia would appreciate considering the long hours she worked.

Spending every Saturday in a posh jeweller's shop in Piccadilly was something I couldn't quite understand, especially as my sister already worked a five-day week and had an additional career in part-time modelling. Either she was Saturday-working in order to avoid being in her mother's company or she was saving up enough money for her rumoured marriage.

No doubt I'll hear about it when it's actually on the cards, and no doubt Her Ladyship's personal tailor will make his appearance sooner or later, I surmised.

In the meantime and due to the complicated love life I was experiencing, I also gave my mother a wide berth for fear of having to explain myself to her. The trouble was, her past experiences with Sylvia had conditioned her to such a degree that it was almost impossible to hide anything from her. She even listened in to telephone conversations and read private letters that had been opened "by mistake".

"Your sister is going to have a Christmas wedding, Jimmy. Won't it be lovely to see her in a bridal gown in the snow?"

The excitement written across my mother's face not only signified the beginnings of what to her would be an ambition-filled occasion, you could tell that her mind was already ticking its way towards a goal that had long been envisaged. Whether it was because of my sister's imminent departure to another country or her forthcoming marriage to her handsome Frenchman, I wasn't sure, but what became so noticeable was the atmosphere in the home; the climate appeared unusually relaxed. The squabbling seemed to cease, and this was something that didn't happen too often. My sister even attempted to fill the lounge with her singing. Although not one of her strong points, Sylvia did on occasions sing along with the radio, especially when there was a song she liked playing, such as Frankie Vaughan's 'Behind the Green Door' or Guy Mitchell's 'Singing the Blues'. From my perspective I was just glad that my sister had at last decided to settle down and, even though there would be miles and miles between us, the fact that she had found happiness seemed priceless.

***

It was as if a beautiful angel had descended to earth, dressed as a bride! That, in my opinion, was the best way to sum up the appearance of my sister as she began the short walk along the cobblestoned ginnel, a narrow pathway that served as a connection between the noisy suburban streets and the quiet, peaceful enclave of the church. Her white outfit outshone the grey skies and the cobblestones, and her smile reflected a ray of assurance that was heart-warming.

My next sighting of my sister was inside the church, where, having parted company with her father, she met her fiancé for the rituals of the wedding ceremony. Absorbed as I was in my surroundings and the events that were taking place in front of me, I couldn't help but reflect on the activities that had taken place since daybreak, when, following an early breakfast and a moment of calm, the house had burst into life with the arrival of Pierre and his family, including his sister, mother and father. Unfortunately with Pierre being the only member of his family to speak English, a situation arose whereby every question and instruction between my parents and his parents needed deciphering. This was a little awkward, but nevertheless it gave rise to a welcome sense of humour. But proving to be more difficult and embarrassing was the atmosphere in the lounge whenever Pierre left the room; conversation was substituted with forced smiles and cumbersome attempts at chit-chat, including improvised hand signals.

Similar in age to my own parents, the groom's mother and father, who had travelled from their home in Switzerland, not only showed their approval of Sylvia, according to Pierre, they hoped my sister's influence would have the effect of curbing his wanderlust tendencies. For my part, I couldn't fathom how that was going to work, especially knowing of Pierre's commitments as a film cameraman and the exotic locations he was required to travel to. Maybe Sylvia would be accompanying him on his travels and, quite possibly, she would come into contact with the famous film stars Pierre associated with…

A loud blast of organ music interrupted my daydreaming and the chiming church bells indicated the wedding finale. So I hurriedly made my way to the church door in readiness for the execution of my well-planned surprise – the release of a large bag of confetti I had hung above the doorway which, with any luck, would shower the happy couple at exactly the right moment.

Just how well my plan had worked became evident as I arrived at the posh-looking hotel that overlooked Piccadilly Gardens, where, having traced the giveaway confetti trail to my sister, I was able to offer my congratulations. Jokingly, I mentioned the fact that not only had she escaped from Her Ladyship's clutches, it would now be me who would have to endure the aftermath of her departure.

To say that I felt out of place would be an understatement. The grandiose surroundings made me feel out of my depth and I felt myself yearning for an escape to somewhere less intimidating, a place such as the picturesque picnic area that was a feature of one of my countryside bicycling routes.

Fortunately, when it came to the longed-for wedding dinner, I found myself seated alongside my younger sister and her husband – a couple who, like me, were more down to earth and unaffected by the pomp and glitz of the occasion.

"I must admit, Jimmy, Mrs Seymour has good taste when it comes to fashion!"

My sister's avoidance of the word 'mother' was something I fully understood, especially considering the rift and the jealousies that existed between them. As I was unsure whether or not my sister knew about my mother's personal tailor, I remained quiet, but there was no doubting that Her Ladyship's grey suit and matching hat – not forgetting the mink stole – had left an impression on all her guests. Tickled by a thought that had suddenly come to mind, I began wondering whether or not – now that Sylvia would no longer be with us – the familiar Yorkshire tailor with his comical "Mrs Seymour-Smythe" would become a relic of the past; in which case, I for one would be the first to miss his jovial personality.

Sitting at the opposite table to me was a person who was my sister's best friend and bridesmaid. She, above every girl I had ever known, stood out as being the most sincere and kindest of people and, unlike Sylvia, a person whose feet were firmly planted on terra firma. As she caught my gaze, she waved at me and it was at that point that my sister Vera interrupted.

"If it wasn't for Rose, our Sylvia wouldn't be going through with this marriage. She's the one who got them together in the first place."

Whether it was the glass of wine that had stirred my sister's feelings, I couldn't be sure, but having made that point, a further testimony to Rose's common sense, she began revealing the details of Sylvia and Roses' firm friendship. What surprised me was Vera's in-depth knowledge of the situation. Unlike me, she appeared to know everything about Sylvia's private life, including the failed affair with the Polish doctor.

"I never met him but even Rose, her best friend, thought they were well suited. Pity that Mrs Seymour stuck her nose in and ruined it!" Vera said.

With curiosity getting the better of me, especially as I had always wondered about the doctor's disappearance, I asked Vera what had happened.

"You may not believe it, Jimmy, but because she didn't want them to be together, she actually rang the doctor and told him about Sylvia having been adopted and that her real mother was in an asylum, owing to there being mental illness in the family."

There was a short pause while I struggled to digest this new revelation.

Then my sister, demonstrating the hatred she felt towards my mother, continued, "Did Sylvia ever tell you about that episode concerning her and her real father? It's preyed on her mind ever since it happened. And so guilty does she feel about it; she knows only too well that she's got to live with it."

Not knowing what to say or what to expect, I anxiously waited for her to continue.

She said, "When our Sylvia attended that Manchester High School, she used to meet up with our Dad on his way home from work. He was a typesetter for the Daily Express newspaper. Did you know that? Well, anyway, it was because of Mrs Seymour's jealousy of their continued relationship that she made her tell her father that he wasn't to meet her at her school any more. The excuse Mrs Seymour gave was that her father's smelly work overalls were contaminating Sylvia's expensive school uniform – a reason that, to my mind, was totally pathetic." The anger in my sister's voice was unmistakable. "To think that our father had survived a 'gassing' in the First World War, and paid all his dues whilst we were in care, only to have that thrown in his face."

This additional disclosure stunned me into silence. I found it difficult to believe that my adopted mother could have gone to such devious and deceptive lengths. As I looked towards my just-married sister, knowing what I now knew, I felt great sadness and I secretly hoped that Sylvia and her husband would escape as far away as possible – anywhere away from her mother's influences.

***

Unlike past Christmases when the main focus of attention would have been my sister's partying, I now found myself attracting the same level of scrutiny that Sylvia would have received. My mother wanted to know everything about my social life; she even tried to involve herself and offer advice.

Being no match for her guile, I found myself giving in to most of her suggestions - such as inviting my friends from the operatic society for Saturday or Sunday-evening get-togethers, some of which included hot suppers or Christmas fare. This arrangement suited Her Ladyship as she could get to know who my friends were, but I still managed to hide some things from her - for example, two secret girlfriends about whom she knew nothing.

As a result of the long history of mistrust between her and Sylvia it was inevitable that my mother would display a wariness second to none concerning our own relationship.

"A new year and a new tactic!" I muttered under my breath.

Having summed up my mother's latest strategy as being akin to having enrolled a minder, I knowingly accepted her suggestion of strengthening the friendship that existed between me and one of our neighbour's sons – a boy who was my senior and who resided with his mother. From my point of view the suggestion – much like the motorbike he owned – was like dangling a carrot in front of a mule; it was a titbit I couldn't wait to savour, especially with the warmer springtime weather approaching. In my opinion, what my mother was really trying to get across to me was the fact that the neighbour's son had chosen to devote his spare time to looking after his mother rather than having girlfriends. This became evident when she drew my attention to a particular piece of music that she had placed on the piano – something that "just happened to have caught her eye" whilst shopping.

"It's the 'Maid of the Mountains'. I thought you and your friends would appreciate it," she said.

What she failed to mention was the fact that she had already opened the musical score and the page that was peering at me from above the piano keys was headed 'A bachelor gay'.

This wasn't the first time I had heard this song mentioned, it being a favourite of my mother's and one that on occasions I had heard her try to sing, albeit out of tune. The fact that the song was supposed to imply a message was obvious as rarely did she present something to me without there being a reason for it. Every word of the song seemed to spell it out:

> "At seventeen, he falls in love quite madly with eyes of a distant blue;
> At twenty-four he gets it rather badly – with eyes of a different hue,
> At thirty-five you'll find him flirting sadly – with two, or three or more –
> When he fancies he is passed love it is then he meets his last love – and he loves her as he's never loved before."

What my mother didn't know was that my life was about to change and that instead of the so-called 'mummy's boy' she yearned for, I was about to embark on a life-changing career that involved countrywide travel. Although luck had played its part, if it hadn't been for my night-school studies and a determination to better myself, the opportunity may never have arisen. As it was, the boredom and lack of promotion at my place of work had prompted me to look elsewhere and, following several failed attempts to obtain a position, I at last received the news I had hoped for – an invitation to an interview in the city of London.

Once my parents had come to terms with the fact

that I was one step away from being a 'commercial traveller', car included, they began to sing my praises and congratulate my achievement. They manifested their pride by informing all their friends and acquaintances of their son's promotion.

"Now don't forget your manners, Jimmy; talk nicely and be on your best behaviour. Let them see that you've been brought up well and that you're a gentleman."

With those words still fresh in my mind and the image of my mother fussing over my appearance as she saw me off from the doorstep, I eventually claimed my carriage seat on the London-bound express train where, alone with my thoughts, I went through the process of reassuring myself that everything about today was real.

By the end of my training week - a period in which I succeeded in every task - I earned the reward of becoming the company's newest recruit and was handed the keys to a gleaming new car, which, now filled with many shoe-product samples, I couldn't wait to drive back to Manchester.

With my excitement slowly evaporating, I settled down to concentrate on the long journey ahead. As my thoughts meandered, I recalled the proud moment when I was told by the managing director that my job success had been down to the letter-writing abilities I had demonstrated in my application. Then my thoughts turned to the more pleasing aspect of my stay in a hotel - my leisure time, which, if it hadn't been for the attractive chambermaid, would probably have been a mundane and boring experience.

I can just picture that first moment of contact when, on the second evening of my stay and following my return from head office, I found her sitting on my bed with a needle and cotton in her hand. That she was young and pretty was obvious, and she told me that she had just finished sewing two buttons onto my shirt, for which I thanked her. Whether it was down to her Irish accent or the fact that she was naturally friendly, I wasn't sure, but following an introduction and a flirtation of sorts, she eventually planted a kiss on my cheek before exiting the room.

With that close contact still on my mind and following my return from yet another day of learning, I sat myself on the bed in anticipation of Eileen's knock on the door, my mind filled with fantasies.

Not until ten o'clock that evening did she show her face, but it was just a quick "hello" as I enjoyed my supper in the hotel lounge.

"You weren't expecting me to come to the bedroom this evening, were you?"

"No," I replied, hoping she wouldn't detect my disappointment.

"Sorry, I can't stop now; I've got a friend waiting for me. How about us going for a drink tomorrow evening?"

Without any hesitation whatsoever, and under the spell of those delicate fingers that were now massaging my neck, I responded with an overjoyed, "Yes, of course!"

With one last gesture before departing, she leaned close to my ear and whispered, "Don't forget to bring 'you know what' with you."

Having interpreted her 'you know what' to be a way of reminding me about taking precautions, I went to bed that night thinking not only of the pleasure that lay in store but also of tomorrow's lunchbreak and the challenge I would face in trying to purchase a Durex.

Having succeeded in my quest and this being my final evening prior to taking receipt of my new vehicle, it was little wonder that my excitement was beginning to get the better of me, especially with my rendezvous with Eileen just minutes away.

She announced her arrival by way of a kiss on my cheek and then asked me to fetch her a drink and a packet of ten cigarettes from the hotel bar, a request I willingly obliged – albeit in the hope that, having checked my money situation, she didn't ask for a repeat.

Not since my days in the army had I smoked a cigarette and having decided to share one with her, I was reminded that none of my previous girlfriends had ever smoked, let alone drunk alcohol.

Whether that had something to do with what now came to mind, I wasn't sure, but as I observed Eileen's profile from close up, I was reminded of an incident that had occurred at the time of leaving my childhood institution, a moment in my life when I had come face-to-face with a woman who not only smoked but wore long trousers, just as men did.

Smiling to myself as I recalled meeting that bus 'clippy' all those years ago, I remembered just how naïve I had been about life in general. Perhaps it was the similarity of the mannish, square-shouldered jacket that Eileen was wearing that was making her less appealing, either that or her overdone make-up?

On finishing her drink, she stubbed out her cigarette on the floor prior to linking her arm with mine.

"Are we ready to go now, James?"

"Yes," I answered, undeterred by my thoughts.

Having crossed the main road into what appeared to be public parkland, dotted with trees, shrubs and pathways, I found myself being guided towards a route that was off the beaten track and out of sight. It reminded me of a secret hideaway. A few steps further and inside a darkened enclosure, Eileen detached herself from me and leaned provocatively with her back against a tree trunk, a gesture that implied that this was the moment.

What happened next was something quite unexpected as, no sooner had I leaned towards her than she said, "Haven't you forgotten something?"

My first thought was that she either wanted me to prove that I had come prepared or that she herself wanted to take part in the cautionary procedure.

As I produced the packet of rubbers from my pocket, her attitude changed completely and she loudly exclaimed, "What's this? Are you trying to be funny? Where's my money?"

As the penny dropped, I suddenly realised how naïve I had been in thinking that Eileen had taken a fancy to me. Now she was exhibiting nothing more than the business-like manner of a prostitute. The trouble was, having realised my predicament, I remembered I had very little money on me, and what I did have was earmarked for tomorrow's journey back home.

With her sixth sense spelling out the situation and having readied herself for her departure, she glared at me as if I was a stupid imbecile. Her farewell included a few choice swearwords, which became imbedded in my mind like a barbed implement. She concluded by adding, "Go back to that little place you come from, and grow up."

Although painful and embarrassing, I had at least learned a lesson – one that hopefully would teach me to be a lot more careful.

Chapter Eleven

The three years that had elapsed since beginning my work as a commercial traveller had not only lived up to my expectations, in retrospect I had lived a life of fulfilment and enjoyed much job satisfaction too. It was more than I could ever have wished for.

Now, with all my travelling – covering an area between the Yorkshire boundaries and the Lancashire coast – I had improved my geographical knowledge and become more mature along the way. Also, I had come to know numerous friends and acquaintances during my travels, including the proprietors of the many hotels I frequented and a variety of company representatives from many trade organisations.

Needless to say, not only had I grown more confident as a person, my life had acquired a status that was comparable to that of anyone who had achieved their ambition in life. Unfortunately, and owing to my success, my mother's overall view of me was one of disappointment - especially on the prickly subject of my socialising, and this resulted in my spending less time in the home.

The advantage of having a car meant that I could occasionally stray from my established circle of close friends, and this led to my meeting a selection of alternative, good-looking female friends whose individuality, intellect and perspective on life was refreshingly different to that of my parents.

One person in particular who caught my eye was a girl named Louise, an attractive black-haired individual whose wit and charm had succeeded in capturing my friendship. And her family were now offering me the same kind of hospitality that would be given to a budding future son-in-law. Considering the genuine and down-to-earth nature of Louise's mother, her family was becoming an attraction that was proving difficult to resist. With a feeling that this relationship could be the one, I began spending more time with Louise. I also came to the decision that now was the time for her to meet my parents – my mother in particular. She, I felt sure, would take to Louise if only because of her sense of fashion – her wide-brimmed floppy hat in particular – and her well-proportioned common sense and optimism.

However, that my mother accepted Louise with surprising good will still threw me off balance. I even began regretting my doubts and suspicions – something that had kept me on tenterhooks since their initial introduction.

Why, I wondered, *after all those years of warnings against becoming involved with girls, is she now changing her tune?*

Perhaps my mother's past reputation was clouding my judgement? Or could it be that in some way she was trying to make up for what had gone on in the past? The best thing to do, I finally decided, was to accept my mother's good will and start looking forward to the future. Needless to say, this thought filled me with huge excitement.

***

"Stupid! Gullible! Idiot!" I growled. *How could I have been so naïve as not to have realised my mother's cunning?*

In the peaceful landscape of the surrounding countryside – my weekend escape from the confines of the city – I relived that fateful day of two weeks ago, trying desperately to come to terms with its evil outcome.

Looking back to the day in question I remembered how full of joy and optimism I had been, especially having achieved success with one of the company's major clients. It was that triumph that had led to my decision to take the scenic route back home, a journey through the countryside that allowed me time to fill my mind with Louise's presence. I also gave some thought to the evening's date I had arranged – a surprise outing to her favourite restaurant.

Without a care in the world and with no hint of what lay in store, I duly arrived at Louise's house where, out of habit, I entered the building via the back door and strode into the kitchen. Such was the level of familiarity between me and the family that I not only sat myself at the table, I also tested the temperature of the teapot in case her mother had prepared a cuppa for me – something she normally did in advance of my visit. The absence of any heat in the pot and the fact that nobody appeared to be around, seemed unusual. When Louise and her mother did show their faces they did so with serious looks, the likes of which were unfamiliar to me. Unfortunately, because of the childhood abuse I'd endured, I had developed an over-sensitive nature; this meant I could smell awkward situations a mile away.

Starting the ball rolling as she sat down, Louise's mother said, "Your mother and I had a long chat this afternoon..."

I knew it! was my silent exclamation, as I proceeded to listen with trepidation to what might be coming next. Even Louise had abandoned her trademark smile.

"I think it's best if you don't see my daughter any more."

My face must have reflected my bitter

disappointment. I replied, "Why? What have I done?"

"It's not that," her mother continued. "You haven't done anything. I just think it's best if you stay away from now on."

Although Louise's sad looks spoke volumes, she continued to remain quiet, almost as if under instructions.

"You're welcome to give Louise a ring now and again but anything else is out of the question. I've said my piece now and that's it. Louise will see you out."

As my disappointment began to take hold, I couldn't help but feel how odd the situation was. My senses were telling me that Louise and I felt the same way about each other, so why did we have to say goodbye?

With a show of sympathy towards me and in an effort to provide some kind of answer, Louise remarked, "It was something your mother said to my mum. I don't want to say any more."

I was determined to know what had transpired and rather than settle for a half-finished explanation, I continued pressing her for the truth.

"Is it true that your real mother is in a mental asylum?"

The shock of what she had said stunned me into silence. I felt a loneliness and a despair that were reminiscent of my past.

"It's not true," I replied. "She's in a workhouse hospital."

On reflection, what I should have said was that my adopted mother was a liar and that the only reason she had exposed my past was so that she could split us up. But it was too late now; the damage had been done and all I wanted to do was be alone with my thoughts

– even if it meant shutting out all of my close friends.

With the weekend imminent and having felt an overwhelming desire to rid myself of my troubled thoughts, I automatically made a beeline for my favourite hillside location. As my anger towards my mother began to subside I gradually gave in to my surroundings – a breath-taking panorama, emblematic of the area I had chosen. Almost as if I had timed it to perfection, the clouds suddenly gave way to brilliant sunshine and a beam of light shone across the valley beneath me. With my attention drawn to the sun's reflection on the distant church spire and my mind having been captured by what seemed the most tranquil of settings, I began the process of putting my life into perspective.

The more I thought, the more the memories came flooding back, especially the ones I shared with my sister. Slowly but surely, and with Sylvia's lingering profile taunting my mind, I began mouthing the lyrics of the 'Jimmy Brown' song:

> "There's a village hidden deep in the valley
> Among the pine trees half forlorn
> And there on a sunny morning
> Little Jimmy Brown was born.
> All the chapel bells were ringing
> In the little valley town
> And the songs that they were singing
> Were for baby Jimmy Brown…"

With the accompaniment of 'All the chapel bells were ringing' echoing in my ears, I returned home in a better mood, and because of it I became more determined about the course of action I would now take.

"I was only trying to protect you."

In an effort to smooth things over and break the deadlock between us, my mother apologised in her own way for what she had said to Louise's mother. But she also continued with her pathetic excuses, as if trying to justify her actions.

"It wouldn't have lasted; she had no breeding – and she certainly wasn't right for you!"

During the weeks that followed, the strained atmosphere continued, and I purposely seized every opportunity to stay out of the house and out of earshot of the caustic comments relating to my behaviour. To say that it was an unhappy house would be an understatement, especially with my father continuing to support his wife. Thank goodness I had an occupation that allowed me to get on with my life, and as I had my own means of transport, I was able to escape frequently. During my escapes, I planned a future that was free from interference and control.

***

Catherine came into my life at a time when I was 'off' girls in general. So it was as if our walk along that same footpath on that particular day had been a collision of destinies. More to the point, however, was the fact that I had accidently become tangled with the lead that was attached to her pet dog. As the poor creature looked up at me with a mournful gaze, it held out one of its front paws, as if wanting to shake hands, which seemed to break the ice.

On exchanging introductions, I became aware of the fact that Cathy was from a different county and was here to visit a relative. She was also due to return home with her parents that very same evening. Why I experienced such a feeling of sadness at the thought of Cathy's departure, I couldn't explain, especially as I had only just met her.

The more I thought about the shy, good-looking girl who had made such an impression on me, the more convinced I became that fate had caused our paths to cross, and this also appealed to my sense of romance.

Not for another three long weeks would we meet up again and when we did, I made sure that I partnered her on her dog walks and asked her for her telephone number – a request she willingly complied with.

Our first kiss – the one that had been building since holding each other's hands for the first time – was more than fulfilling, and I began to realise that Catherine's openness and innocence had thrown me off balance and given rise to a flurry of strong feelings. Could it be that the chemistry between us had worked its magic, or was it the coincidence of both of us having experienced a recent broken romance that made us feel so close?

The thing that pleased me the most – assuming our friendship was destined to blossom – was the fact that Cathy would be in a position to escape my mother's influence as she lived a long way off. Also, because I had explained the situation to her, we had agreed that, in order to keep in touch, I would telephone her either at home or at her place of work.

Since very little escaped my mother, it wasn't long before she fathomed out the reason behind my frequent disappearances, and due to my reluctance to share any details with her, the already strained atmosphere intensified.

It was at this point that I realised I had reached a

crossroads in my life and although it had never entered my mind in the past, I was now beginning to consider the unthinkable – leaving my home forever. I could find a decent bedsit on the other side of the city, a place where I could live my life in my own way.

The decision, when I finally reached it, was an easy one to make. In fact, it was forced on me by something my mother did – something so despicable that I wanted nothing more to do with her, and I hurriedly began removing all of my possessions as quickly as possible from the house.

"To think that not only has she gone behind my back, she has actually contacted my head office in London!" I fumed.

Fortunately, and to my advantage, there had been a timely intervention from my area supervisor who, with prior knowledge of my home circumstances, had offered me a sympathetic ear. He had also gone to the trouble of assuring the sales directors that no further action would be necessary, a kindness for which I would always be grateful.

"In future, don't burn your surplus advertising paraphernalia in your back garden, as you have been doing. Take it to a rubbish dump instead," he advised.

That so-called crime of setting fire to company literature had, in my mother's opinion, been the perfect weapon to achieve not only my sacking from my job but also a way of putting me down.

As I prepared to spend that first night in my one-room apartment, I didn't allow myself to become downhearted by its dark and dismal state; instead I began picturing the improvements I could make – especially in preparation for when Cathy came to visit. But there was one particular feeling I just couldn't ignore; suddenly it was as if all my troubles had been taken from me and replaced with a sense of relief, something I hadn't imagined possible.

"I'm free at last!" I shouted joyfully.

Unfortunately, though, by the time I had pulled the musty-smelling blanket over me, I had already experienced my first feelings of doubt - a mindset that, taking into account the many comments thrown at me when leaving home, had begun to gnaw away at me and the life-changing decision I had made.

"You'll soon get fed up and come crawling back! You'll see!"

The very thought of that happening had made me more determined than ever to stick to my guns, but even as I tried blocking out her words, yet more engulfed me.

"You think you're a big man full of self-importance, don't you? Where would you be now if we hadn't picked you out of the gutter?"

***

Such was the bond between me and Cathy that not only had we become more serious in our relationship, what was taking place now - in this very street and in front of this angry audience – was the result of our decision to get married and buy a home of our own.

"If you're so clever, why don't you take us to court?"

The policeman's look of disgust and my father's strong words made it seem as if I was fighting a losing battle. My sparse legal knowledge made me feel ill-equipped, and the opposition's growing fury caused me to sense inevitable doom.

Stressful though it was, the impasse was brought to

an end by the timely appearance of my parents' solicitor, who having had words with both his clients and the police constable, informed me that an agreement had been reached between him and my solicitor – a "moving forward", as he put it, without the need of any more family encounters.

How ironic was the lawyer's choice of words! The truth was, from that day onwards and for the rest of my life, due to my strong feelings of bitterness, I never again set eyes on my adopted parents and I tried to erase them from my memory.

Although regretting having to spend every last penny I had saved, at least it meant that my parents were able to buy a new home for the two of them. And I too was putting down roots. For the first time ever, I was able to plan my future life without interference. I had finally become responsible for a destiny that was of my own choosing. No longer would I be looking back to the past; the present and the future were where I belonged.

AFTERWORD

Unsurprisingly, a few years after Jimmy's discharge, the 'children's colony' that had caused him so much unhappiness was converted into a prison.

Following a period in later life when his past had caught up with him, Jimmy suffered the trauma of a mental breakdown. It was during this dark period and with the help of yoga – something he had accidently stumbled across - that slowly but surely he began the task of piecing his life together.

The following poem, which he wrote at the time, is a reflection of a mindset that is searching intently for the elusive – if not impossible – meaning to life.

OCEAN OF TEARS

A teardrop fell, and down through the years it sped upon its way,
Gathering momentum through all of life's disarray.
The Sea of Happiness laid claim to it, as did the Darkest Sea too,
This precious tear, so crystal clear, which they both had come to woo.
Brimming with emotions that had accompanied it from the womb,
It experienced both good and bad, along the highway to its tomb.
Goodness, evil and a superior enlightenment about earthly life
Were its witnesses in a never-ending plight of strife.
Until, having perceived every human doubt and fear,
It found its final destiny, a sanctuary – an Ocean of Tears.

THANKS

Many thanks to *peermusic.com* for their kind permission to reproduce some of the lyrics of 'The Jimmy Brown Song':

The Three Bells (The Jimmy Brown Song)

Music and French lyric by Jean Villard / English

Lyrics by Bert Reisfeld

©1945 Les Nouvelles Editions Meridian, France

©1948 Southern Music Publishing Co. Inc., USA

To Laura, Gilda and Malcolm

Whilst the events, locations and conversations remain accurate to my memory, names of the story-line characters - excluding Jimmy Brown, Sylvia and Vera - are totally fictitious. Any resemblance to actual persons, living or dead, is purely co-incidental.